Ruth Mowry Brown

The Bible in Lesson and Story

Ruth Mowry Brown

The Bible in Lesson and Story

ISBN/EAN: 9783337171476

Printed in Europe, USA, Canada, Australia, Japan

Cover: Foto ©Lupo / pixelio.de

More available books at **www.hansebooks.com**

The Bible in Lesson and Story

THE CHRIST-CHILD.
From a painting by Ittenbach.

The Bible in Lesson and Story

For use in Sunday Schools,
Junior Young People's Societies,
and in the Home

By
Ruth Mowry Brown

United Society of Christian Endeavor
Boston and Chicago

Colonial Press:
Electrotyped and Printed by
C. H. Simonds & Co.
Boston, Mass., U. S. A.

TO
THE MEMORY OF MY
Mother
WHOSE LIFE AND TEACHINGS
MADE POSSIBLE THIS LITTLE BOOK

PREFACE.

A WISE man has said, "Give me the first ten years of a child's life, and I care not who has the training of the rest of his life." We may not go so far as to be regardless of the later training, but it is undeniable that what is learned during the years of early childhood gains such a hold upon a child's nature that it cannot be easily obliterated. It is also true that this is the time when right impressions are the most easily produced. This is the golden opportunity for telling the Bible stories. It is a much more important time for impressing the truth that lies back of the story. Too often is the Bible story told in such a way as to give only individual facts to the child rather than to teach the valuable lesson that underlies the tale. In this book the author has endeavored to keep in mind the underlying truth at all points, and to present the lessons in such a manner that the child shall receive the truth, and that it shall delight rather than repel him. Impressed with the necessity of such lessons for her own use with children, the author prepared and used them herself, and now gives them to the public in the hope that others will find them of service.

All children love the story, and the story is one of the most effective means of leading the child in the right way. Children with bright, active minds often object to the "goody-goody" story, or to the constant use of stories with the moral in plain sight. Great pains have been taken to give such stories as shall point the truth of the lesson without offending the child's rights or wounding his natural dignity.

If we would remember that "the Spirit of God moves upon the child's spirit as the ocean sways the seaweed," then we should bend all our energies to bring to the child all the beautiful waves that God has set in motion, and not stand aside and let God's Spirit work alone; much less should we hinder the work. We watch the wave as it lightly moves the seaweed; but we never know where or how far it reaches, or how many other pieces of seaweed it gently sways as it flows on throughout time. We can give to the child some little idea of one of God's wonderful truths, but we cannot follow it through the child's life or know how many other lives it may touch.

If the children can be made to feel something of "God's wonderful power," to know him as God, then a long step has been taken toward reverence, toward love to God, toward right living in general. Miss Wiltse says: "The child sees men and women, fathers, mothers, and children, in the stars; . . . love is the element in which the stars exist. Mother love leads to God love, and the child climbs from his mother's arms beyond the stars, finally reaching the abstract knowledge that only that which is a reflection of God will abide eternally, and that which reflects spirit is spirit. There is a significance in the child's desire to reach the stars which we would better gravely consider than laugh at, either thoughtlessly or contemptuously. The soul that holds its aspirations in spite of all temporary and temporal hindrances will as assuredly find its way back to God as the stars move in their appointed ways. Shall we not rather help than hinder the child's aspirations?"

Jesus Christ said, "The sabbath was made for

man, and not man for the sabbath." Is it not equally true that the Bible was made for man, and not man for the Bible? Then let us select for the children such lessons and stories as shall be of the most benefit to them. Let us omit all tales of bloodshed and horror, all stories of sin, as far as possible; and let us give the children the bright and beautiful which lead to right and noble thoughts and living. Let us fill the children's minds so full of the good and true that there shall be no room for wickedness.

Grateful recognition is made of valuable help received from Mr. and Mrs. Arthur May Mowry, and Miss Margaret McCloskey, who have read the manuscript and offered excellent suggestions. Thanks are also due to the following for their kind permission to use their stories: Elizabeth E. Foulke, and Silver, Burdett & Co., author and publishers of "Twilight Stories"; Harriet A. Cheever, and the Congregational Sunday-School and Publishing Society, author and publishers of "Little Jolliby's Christmas" and "The Fairies of Fern Dingle"; and W. A. Wilde & Co.

SUGGESTIONS.

THESE lessons and stories are equally well adapted for use in the home, where the mother gives them to the children; and in Sunday schools and young people's societies, where the teacher presents the lesson to a class. It is hoped that mothers as well as superintendents will appreciate the suggestions for occupations in connection with the lessons. The author has tried to give directions that shall be plain enough to be easily followed, but the mother or the teacher may often prefer to change the occupation to suit her individual children or her resources. In each lesson the occupation is intended for the children; that is, it is intended that the children shall do the work under the guidance of teacher or mother. For instance, in the lesson on Isaac, let the children build the well. Give each child a block, and direct him where to place it. When the well is built, and the children understand how the water was drawn, let one of the children move up to the well whatever is to be used to represent Abraham's servant; then another child should move toward the well from the other direction whatever represents Rebekah. As to the elaborateness of the figures used to represent persons and different objects, it will depend upon the teacher's resources. Real figures of men can be employed, but children will be just as much interested by the use of a stick of wood with a base to enable it to stand; their imagination will do the rest. The servant can have a camel upon which he is supposed to be riding, or the children can imagine the camel.

There is nothing arbitrary about the use of these objects. The author has given the occupations as suggestions, and has left to the teacher the selection of material. If the lessons are to be used where the occupations are not desired, these can be omitted, as the lessons and stories are complete without them.

It is hoped that the teachers will study the lessons so carefully that they will not only get the thought in mind, but will also acquire something of the childlike style of telling the story, because it is important to make the lesson simple and interesting to the children. Many teachers think the best method is to tell the lesson story first in its fulness, and then go over it again as the children use the objects of the occupation. In this way the children give their whole attention to the telling of the lesson the first time, and are quite inclined to be attentive, as they know that the occupations will follow immediately. This gives the teacher an opportunity to review the various points during the occupation.

The first eight lessons, which relate to the creation, teach God's wonderful power. The stories connected with these lessons illustrate separate truths, as given in the following list. The last thirty-two truths are found in both lesson and story.

TRUTHS.

1. God has wonderful power.
2. God shapes our lives.
3. God is always giving.
4. God's plan is best.
5. Unselfishness brings joy.
6. We cannot know what is best for ourselves.
7. We should be kind to animals.
8. Right living brings happiness.
9. A contented disposition is a blessing.

SUGGESTIONS. 13

10. We should reverence God's law.
11. Sin brings unhappiness.
12. Work is a gift from God.
13. Trifles make perfection.
14. God keeps his promises.
15. God gives new life.
16. We all influence others.
17. Love is a great power.
18. Giving is a pleasure.
19. Brotherly love permits no wrong thoughts.
20. God overrules for our good.
21. Sin leaves a scar.
22. We should give implicit obedience.
23. Laws are necessary.
24. We should have love for God and man.
25. We should reverence God's house.
26. We should show our thankfulness.
27. We should be God's soldiers.
28. We should choose right companions.
29. God answers prayer.
30. We should use our gifts for others.
31. Brotherly love is kind.
32. God is our Shepherd.
33. We should give our best for God.
34. God knows our thoughts.
35. God will provide.
36. We should remember mother's teaching.
37. We should never taste liquor.
38. Christ is needed.
39. Christ is promised.
40. The Christ-child fulfils the promise.

CONTENTS.

LESSON		PAGE
I.	CREATION	21
	Story — The Stone-cutter	24
II.	CLAY	28
	Story — The Story the Vase Told	30
III.	DRY LAND	34
	Story — The Wonderful Story	37
IV.	GROWTH OF PLANTS	40
	Story — The Milkweed Seeds	43
V.	THE SUN, MOON, AND STARS	46
	Story — The Legend of the Diamond Dipper	49
VI.	SEA LIFE	52
	Story — The Three Trouts	54
VII.	ANIMAL LIFE	58
	Story — A Mongrel's Memories	61
VIII.	MAN	65
	Story — Philly's Fairies	67
IX.	CONTENTMENT	71
	Story — Suppose	74
X.	THE SEVENTH DAY	77
	Story — Carl's Sunday	79
XI.	SIN	86
	Story — The Fairy and the Gnome	83
XII.	WORK	89
	Story — Amy Stewart	92
XIII.	CAIN AND ABEL	94
	Story — The Immortal Fountain	97

CONTENTS.

LESSON		PAGE
XIV.	NOAH	102
	Stories — The Rainbow Pilgrimage	105
	Iris Bridge	107
XV.	EASTER	109
	Story — The Wonderful Change	112
XVI.	ABRAHAM	115
	Story — Rupert's Dream	118
XVII.	ISAAC	122
	Story — The Children's Hour	125
XVIII.	JACOB	127
	Stories — In Heaven	130
	Star Dollars	130
XIX.	JOSEPH THE BOY	132
	Story — The Lily-Pipe	135
XX.	JOSEPH THE RULER	139
	Story — Sulky Sibyl	142
XXI.	JOSEPH'S BRETHREN	144
	Story — The Hitching-Post	147
XXII.	MOSES	150
	Story — Just as Well	153
XXIII.	THE WILDERNESS	156
	Story — The Daisy Dance	159
XXIV.	THE TEN COMMANDMENTS	162
	Story — Which Loved Best?	165
XXV.	THE TABERNACLE	167
	Story — May at Church	170
XXVI.	JOSHUA	173
	Story — God Will Know	176
XXVII.	THE FALL OF JERICHO	178
	Story — A True Soldier	180
XXVIII.	RUTH	184
	Story — Master Don't-Want-To	187
XXIX.	SAMUEL	190
	Story — Mary's Daily Bread	193
XXX.	DAVID AND SAUL	195
	Story — The Bird and the Smile	197
XXXI.	DAVID AND JONATHAN	200
	Story — Spot, Smut, and Sly	202

CONTENTS.

LESSON		PAGE
XXXII.	THE SHEPHERD PSALM	206
	Story — The Lost Sheep	209
XXXIII.	SOLOMON'S TEMPLE	210
	Story — Joe's Lily	213
XXXIV.	SOLOMON'S PROVERBS	216
	Story — Thought Echoes	218
XXXV.	ELIJAH	221
	Story — The Open Door	223
XXXVI.	THE LITTLE MAID	226
	Story — A Japanese Story	229
XXXVII.	DANIEL	233
	Story — Nat's Decision	236
XXXVIII.	ISAIAH	239
	Story — Little Jolliby's Story	242
XXXIX.	JOHN	245
	Story — The New Song	247
XL.	THE BABE JESUS	250
	Story — Glory to God	253

ILLUSTRATIONS.

The Christ-Child . . . . . *Frontispiece*
    From a painting by Ittenbach.
Golden Leaves . . . . . *Facing Page* 40
    From a painting by J. E. Grace.
Peace Be to This House 65
    From a painting by Dobson.
The Guardian Angel 83
    From a painting by B. Plockhorst.
Madonna and Child 94
    From a painting by Roberto Ferruzzi.
Rebecca at the Well 122
    From a painting by Frederick Goodall.
Finding of Moses 150
    From a painting by Delaroche.
Ruth 184
    From a painting by Brück-Lajos.
The Good Shepherd 206
    From a painting by B. Plockhorst.
The Pitcher of Tears 221
    From a painting by Paul Thumann.
St. John and the Lamb . . . 245
    From a painting by Murillo.
Holy Night 250
    From a painting by Havenith.

THE
BIBLE IN LESSON AND STORY.

LESSON I.

CREATION.

"*I am God, and there is none else.*" — Isa. 45 : 22.

A LONG time ago, long before your papa can remember, or your grandpa either, so long ago even that no person was living, there were no houses or fences, no churches or schoolhouses. No trees, no plants, no grass, no dirt, no rocks, were to be seen. No animals roamed the earth; no birds flew in the air; no fish swam in the sea. No sounds of living beings were to be heard. There were no floating clouds, no bright stars, no pretty moon. The beautiful sun did not shine, and no snow or rain fell. No light shone through the darkness. There was no land or water, no earth such as we live upon. Our world did not exist. All was quiet and still.

There was but one thing living anywhere in all space, and that was God. No one else existed, and he had all power and wisdom and might. He had always been, and always will be. He was not like man, who must eat and drink and sleep, and who gets tired. He was God. He knew everything, and had such power as we cannot understand. He could make a beautiful world like ours. He could create the stars and sun and moon. He could make the grass and trees grow. He could make men and women and little children. Time made no difference to him, for he had been from everlasting and will be forever; and therefore he need not hurry or hasten in anything. Thus, when God made this beautiful, wonderful earth upon which we now live, he was in no haste to have it finished. It was years and years, thousands of years, in making, and ages and ages in becoming ready for man to live upon; and God wished it to be so. God knew all the wonderful things that should be upon this earth, and he planned them all for the good of men and women and the dear little children who he knew would sometime live here.

We do not know very much about the beginning of the world, but in the Bible it says: "In the beginning God created the heaven and the earth. And the earth was waste and void; and darkness was upon the face of the deep." We do not know how long a time this took, but we may be sure that God did not hurry his work. All was done in the best possible manner. · This was the beginning. There was nothing before this except God, and he had always been. In the beginning God created. Did he have any help? No, God alone did it. There was none other. God was all there was; and, had there been any other, he could not have helped God. God had all power, and so needed no help.

The earth which God made in the beginning did not look as it does now. No one lived on it, or could live on it, as it was then. It was also all dark. Shut your eyes tight, and think of this great mass without shape or life, and covered with darkness. We should not have cared to be there, should we? It must have been a most strange and gloomy place.

Then God said, " Let there be light : and there

CREATION.

was light. And God saw the light that it was good: and God divided the light from the darkness. And God called the light Day, and the darkness he called Night." How wonderful a thing the light is! This world would seem very strange if we were obliged to grope about in darkness all the time. We should not be as happy if there were no light. We could not see the beautiful fleecy clouds sail across the blue sky, nor the lovely shades of green of the trees and grass. The white, red, pink, and blue of the flowers would all be the same to us. We should know the flowers only by our touch and their smell. Thus, when God spoke, the wonderful light appeared. God knew how great a pleasure it would be to us. We do not know how long a time the day was or how long the darkness lasted. The time when it was light God called day, and the time of the darkness he called night. It was not like our day and night, nor like our light from the sun. God planned it all as it should be, and he saw that it was all good.

MEMORY GEM.

Like a cradle rocking, rocking,
    Silent, peaceful, to and fro,
Like a mother's sweet looks dropping
    On the little face below,
Hangs the green earth, swinging, turning,
    Jarless, noiseless, safe, and slow;
Falls the light of God's face bending
    Down and watching us below.
                  — *Saxe Holm.*

OCCUPATION.

Have the children close their eyes and try to imagine the world as it was without regular shape and in darkness. When the children realize that only God could make the world, then illustrate by soap-bubbles. Blow only one at a time. Contrast the imperishableness of the world and the frailty of the bubble. Compare the irregular darkness of the earth with the regular shape and beautiful colors of the soap-bubble, and speak of the later beauty of the earth. Illustrate by the easily moved bubble God's power in guiding the earth. Bring out the fact that God's power in doing this is continuous and even; that the earth is not like the floating bubble blown here and there by the breath. Illustrate God's wonderful power by the fact that the making of this great world was to him no more than the blowing of a bubble to the children.

The chief point of this lesson is to impress God's wonderful power, his might and wisdom.

Directions for Preparing a Soap-bubble Mixture.

Put into a pint bottle two ounces of the best white Castile soap, cut into thin shavings, and fill the bottle with cold water which has been first boiled and then left to cool. Shake well together, and allow the bottle to stand until the upper part of the solution is clear. Decant this solution; use two parts and add one part of glycerine. This should make a bubble that with care will last some time.

STORY.—THE STONE-CUTTER.

A stone-cutter was at work one day patiently chiselling away on a stone. Thud, thud, thud went the hammer upon the chisel. Hum, hum, hum went the man's thoughts. "How tired I am of chiselling away at this stone all day long and day after day!" Just then the sound of trumpets was heard, and the man left his work to watch a great procession go by; the king was travelling through the country in state, and all the people had stopped their work to see him. "I wish I were the king," thought the stone-cutter; "then I should no longer be obliged to pound, pound, pound all day."

No sooner had he thought this than he found himself the king, and was being driven through the country, receiving homage wherever he went. As he journeyed south, it became very warm and the heat was most uncomfortable. Awnings were arranged to shield him from the sun, but he still found the heat almost unbearable. "Why should I, the king of all this great country, be annoyed and made uncomfortable by the heat of the sun, and not be able to prevent it? It must be that the sun is more powerful than I am. I do not wish anything to be stronger than I. I wish I were the sun."

At once the stone-cutter became the sun, and was shining down upon the already hot earth with unusual heat. The ground became parched and dry, and the plants and crops began to die. The people looked troubled, and wondered how long the terrible heat would continue. The stone-cutter, who had now become the sun, felt that he was the most powerful thing in the world, and was happy. Soon, however, clouds began to gather, and the sun was hidden, and could no longer send its hot rays to the earth. The rain began to fall upon the dry and dusty earth; and the stone-cutter, hidden behind the clouds, heard the glad exclamations of the people when the cooling rain refreshed the hot land. "Surely," he said to himself, "the rain is more powerful than the sun. Would I were the rain instead of the sun."

Immediately the stone-cutter became the rain, and felt very happy in the thought of how much good he was doing. But many of the drops fell into the ocean and were lost in its depths. Then the stone-cutter said: "The ocean is more powerful than the rain even, since the rain falls on the water, and is at once lost. I will be the ocean."

The stone-cutter found himself the mighty ocean. During a storm it would rise high and dash over rocks, but it could not move the solid bowlders. It beat hard and long against them, but they stood immovable. "These rocks are more powerful than the ocean; I wish I were the mighty rocks."

Then the stone-cutter became the rock, and stood firm and calm as the waves dashed against its hard sides. At length, however, a stone-cutter came and began to chisel the great rock, and soon it was broken in pieces. "The stone-cutter is mightier than the stone he cuts. I should have done better to remain a stone-cutter." Again the stone-cutter found himself chiselling away at the rock, thud, thud, thud. He no longer was dissatisfied, but he continued to think.

"I have been all these mighty and powerful things, but each time I found something more powerful than I. Now I am a stone-cutter again. I have power over the rock because I can break it in pieces, but I cannot make the rock. I cannot make the rain fall. I cannot make the sunshine. There must be a power so much greater than any other as to rule all these mighty things."

Just at this time a shower came up, and the thunder was very loud, and the flash of the lightning unusually bright. As the thunder rolled and reverberated through the clouds, it seemed to the stone-cutter as if God's voice were speaking to him and saying: "The thunder rolls at my command; the lightning flashes at my word. I hold the waves in the hollow of my hand, and the rock is to me no stronger than a tiny shell. The loftiest mountains are to me as small mounds and as easily moved. Man himself was made by my hand, and given a mind that he might understand that I am God and that I have all power and strength. I gave him also a heart, that, knowing my strength and goodness, he might love and serve me with all his heart and soul, with all his mind and strength. I am God. I have been from everlasting, and shall be forever. All things were made by my hand, and without me was not anything made that is made."

LESSON II.
CLAY.

" We are the clay, and thou our potter; and we all are the work of thy hand." — Isa. 64: 8.

At the time we have been talking about, so many thousands of years ago, the world looked very different from what it does now. God was going to make parts of the earth like a beautiful garden. At this time, however, he had not made the great forests of trees, nor the beautiful flowers. No birds sung, and no butterflies flitted about. But the loving God knew that he would later send little children to live here, and he had a great many things to make ready for them.

At this time, so long ago, there were great oceans; and the oceans were larger than they are now, and covered the rocks; and because there was little land there were few rivers. Then the rocks began to rise above the water; and, as the land became larger, the rivers became greater in size and strength, and there were more of them. As the rivers grew stronger, they began to tear away pieces of rock and roll them down the mountains and hills. These rocks would bump against other rocks and break up into small pieces; they would roll along the river-bed, and dig that deeper and deeper. The rocks were pounded together by the force of the water, and became smaller and smaller, until they were ground to powder finer than flour.

With some of this fine powder ground from the rocks other things were mixed, until it made a kind of earth which after a time was ready for plants to grow in; some was made into sand such as you find by the ocean; some of it was carried by the water into low places in the earth, and then it was laid to rest on cool, dark beds, where it lay damp and hidden for thousands of years, until at last it became clay. Not all the rock was pounded up in this way, for much of it was left for us to build into strong houses and walls. But God wished also to have the soil upon which could grow plants and vegetables for us to eat, and land where we could build houses to live in.

I cannot tell you of all that was done for us before we came; but you shall hear of more wonderful things than this at another time; now we are to talk only about the powdered stones that lay in these beds under water so long, but were finally lifted up into the clear sunlight.

Who can tell me what color clay is? Yes, most of it is gray; but there are also blue, white, red, and yellow clays. I have seen cliffs all streaked through with red, black, yellow, brown, and white clays.

Can we use clay for anything besides moulding pretty shapes, — spheres and pears and animals? Sometimes clay is mixed with sand and made into bricks, which are then burnt in a hot fire to make them hard. We use the bricks to make houses. God knew we should use them in this way.

There are several different kinds of clay. A fine clay is baked to make pots and pans, and is called potter's clay. The Bible speaks of the potter's using the clay, and says that we are like clay, and that God is our potter. He shapes and moulds our lives just as you press the clay to make it of a beautiful form. God plans and shapes our lives to make them more beautiful. "We are all the work of his hands." He made the clay, and he just as truly made us. We belong to him, and should not fret if we cannot do just as we please; for God knows how to make the best men and women of us.

There is a clay still finer than the potter's clay, which is called kaolin or china clay, and is used in making the finest and most beautiful china. Great pains is taken to shape the finer clay into beautiful forms. Which would you rather be like, the clay that is made into pots and kettles or that which is made into handsome china, and requires more pressing and moulding? Would you not rather that God should make your lives good and beautiful, even if you cannot always do what you like? We cannot make our own lives better unless we are willing to let God do as he sees best. We could not have made the soft clay from the hard stone. (Show a piece of granite.) Was it not kind of God to do for us what we cannot do for ourselves?

MEMORY GEM.

Take my feet, and let them be
Swift and beautiful for thee;
Take my voice, and let me sing
Always, only, for my King.
— *Frances R. Havergal.*

OCCUPATION.

Give each child a lump of clay with which to make pots and jars. Show the children how to mould it into the shape of a vase. Various specimens of pottery shown to the children will add to the interest.

STORY.— THE STORY THE VASE TOLD.

Dorothy had been playing so hard that she was very tired and lay down on the lounge to rest. She did not know what to do with herself, and exclaimed, "O dear! I wish some one would tell me a story."

"I will tell you one, if you would like," said a soft voice above her.

Dorothy looked all about to see who had spoken, but could see no one.

"Here I am on the mantel," and Dorothy glanced up to see the large vase on the corner of the mantel looking down as if smiling upon her.

"O do! I never heard of a vase telling a story. What will you tell me about?"

"I will tell you a story about myself. I have lived a long time and seen a great many things. The first I remember was lying in a big bed way down under the water. I had no blankets such as you have, but I needed none. I did wish to be able to look about more, but still there was much to be seen even under the water. I saw many things that you do not know about. I could tell you many interesting stories of the strange animals that lived near me. I remained in this deep, dark bed a great many years, until by and by I was no longer covered by water, but lay in the bright, warm sunshine. Everything was new and strange to me. Instead of the sound of rippling water there were the song of birds and the hum of insects. Sometimes sweet odors came floating toward me from a place where I could see green trees. All these things were so beautiful that I did not grow tired of lying in the sunlight. I did not look as I do now, but was simply a lump of clay lying with a great deal more of the same material. I cannot tell you how long I lay there; for I do not know, and you could not understand so long a time. You have lived only a few years, and I lay there many hundred times as long as your whole life.

"At last, one day, a man came and dug me out of

the bed where I had lain so long, and carried me off with ever so much more of the clay about me. I never had travelled before, and was so surprised that I hardly knew what was happening to me. All I remember was that I was put inside of a building with more clay; and, when I had become rested after my journey, I was again picked up and pressed and moulded and laid on a round, flat wheel which a man turned round and round. He used his foot to keep the wheel turning, and he pressed his hands on me as I lay on the wheel, pushing in at the bottom and toward the top. Faster and faster went the wheel, and I grew tall and slender, with beautiful curved sides. Sometimes he would stop the wheel and look at me on all sides, and then go to work again.

"After a time he began to make a hole inside, which grew larger and larger as he pressed on the inside, while he kept his other hand on the outside to keep me in shape. Soon the inside of me was in the form that you see I have now. Then I was taken off the wheel and put upon a shelf, while the man placed another piece of clay upon the wheel and moulded it as he had moulded me; but, when it was all done, the vase was of an entirely different shape, but just as beautiful. I watched the man place this by my side, and was happy to have a friend to talk with; for I supposed we were both finished and should stand upon that shelf some time, at least. Then another man came and took me down, and carried me to his work-bench where he carefully cut figures in my soft sides. He made the most beautiful pictures upon me. You can see them now; for, although I went through much after he made these lovely patterns on my sides, every mark that he made is still to be seen.

"When he had finished, I surely thought I was as beautiful as was possible; but I soon found that more was to be done for me. I was placed in a kind of oven, called a kiln, and a hot fire was built beneath me. It was very hot, and I feared that I should lose my beautiful shape or the handsome pattern that the man had cut upon my side. It grew hotter and hotter until I could not tell what was happening to me; but at last it began to grow cold, and finally I was taken out and again set upon a shelf. Then I had time to see that I had lost neither my shape nor the design cut upon me. I also heard the man say: 'There is no reason why this vase will not hold water now. It has a handsome pattern, and is worth painting and enamelling.'

"Was it possible that anything more could be done to make me more beautiful? If so, I was willing; therefore, when another man carried me to his bench, I was glad. He worked very slowly and carefully, giving me a touch of one color here and another there, and finally putting a wash of some strange substance all over me; and I was again put into the kiln and baked. The fire was even hotter than before, but I was glad, because I now felt sure that all this was done to me in order that I might be of more value because of my beauty. I was carried to one or two places before I came here to stand upon this corner of the mantel. I was here before you came to this house, but it seems but a short time to me, as I had lived so much longer before I lived here."

LESSON III.

DRY LAND.

"If thou seek for her as silver, and search for her as for hid treasures." — Prov. 2: 4.

We have talked about the time when there were no birds, nor flowers, nor trees; when there were no men, nor women, nor any little children; when even the big round ball on which we live had not been made. You remember that at first there was only God, and that he made this wonderful earth. God kept changing the earth because he wished sometime to have people live upon it. God took many, many years to do this. In our last lesson we talked about some of these changes. But God was doing other things besides making the clay. He wished to change the earth so that beautiful plants and trees should grow upon it, for he knew that the children and the grown people would like them.

Let us see what the Bible tells us about it.

"God said, Let the waters under the heaven be gathered together unto one place, and let the dry land appear: and it was so. And God called the dry land Earth: and the gathering together of the waters called he Seas: and God saw that it was good."

Before this time the water had been like a dense cloud covering the earth. You know how it looks on a foggy morning. You can hardly see across the street. There was something like this all around the earth. The solid part of the earth kept changing and changing until hills and valleys, mountains and deep places, began to appear. After a time the watery cloud disappeared, and it became water, and filled the hollow places of the earth. If you hold a cold plate over the kettle when the steam is coming from the nose, it will form drops of water on the plate that will run down like a small brook. So the brooks and rivers began to flow down from the higher parts of the earth into the hollows, thus making ponds and lakes and oceans.

As the streams rushed quickly down the hillsides they carried with them little particles of earth, which were left in other places. In this manner the outside of the earth was ever changing, until at length it became ready for plants to grow upon it. There were mosses, ferns, and other simple plants. These grew fast, and soon became very large. A great many ferns grew, some of which were as tall as trees.

Think of great forests of tree ferns. There were also high pines, much taller than any we have now. These grew in deep hollows near rivers and lakes, and little by little filled them up. The ground sunk down, and other plants grew on the top. Often the roots of trees still remained in the soil just as they grew, so slowly and easily did it all settle. Even the light seeds of the plants did not blow away. Thus forest after forest grew and sunk into the earth, only to be followed by others. Big rocks pressed these down, and the whole mass was heated and pressed again until it was changed into hard black stone, which still showed here and there the shape of palm or fern. This took many, many years. What do you suppose this hard black material was? Yes, it was coal. There it lay, year after year, age after age, for there were no people on the earth to find it. Hills rose above those great beds of black stone. Other trees and plants grew, and the world looked very different from what it did at first. God knew that by and by, when men and women and children lived upon the earth, they would be cold in the winter unless they had fires to keep them warm. He knew that they would need this coal with which to build the fires. He planned so many good things for us that we have not found them all out even yet. There were very many useful and very many beautiful things that God wished us to have, and he was at work getting some of these ready for us.

MEMORY GEM.

And Nature, the old nurse, took
    The child upon her knee,
Saying, " Here is a story-book
    Thy Father has written for thee.

" Come, wander with me," she said,
    " Into regions yet untrod;
And read what is still unread
    In the manuscripts of God."

And he wandered away and away
    With Nature, the dear old nurse,
Who sang to him night and day
    The rhymes of the universe.

And whenever the way seemed long,
    Or his heart began to fail,
She would sing a more wonderful song,
    Or tell a more marvellous tale.
                — *Henry W. Longfellow.*

OCCUPATION.

If possible, show the children how steam is condensed into water, and thus illustrate the formation of rivers and seas, and the separation of land from water. By means of a sand-board make a portion of the earth's surface with its irregularities, its depressions and elevations. Have a part of the board free from sand to represent the ocean; and string can be used for the rivers, two or three streams merging into one before they reach the ocean. Use tiny needles of fir or hemlock for the vegetable growth, and illustrate the forming of coal-beds by layer after layer of needles. Have a little of the sand scattered over the needles before another layer is allowed to grow.

STORY.—THE WONDERFUL STORY.

Once there was a father who wrote a wonderful book of stories for his children. The book was so written that it would please every child. If one boy loved animals, he had only to look into his father's book and find the most interesting stories of dogs and horses, of birds and butterflies. There were beautiful stories of flowers, — of the daisy with its golden heart, of the pansy with its blossom like a face, of the four-o'clock that remained shut until afternoon, and many other curious flowers.

There were fairy stories of caves and grottoes, the walls of which were covered with pearls and shells with lovely tints. There were chairs of amber with soft mossy cushions resting on a floor made of sand as white as snow; there were other stories of gardens in which were sea-anemones, starfish, and all kinds of seaweed. In this book were stories of the ocean with its hills and valleys all hidden under the dancing waves. There were many other stories so wonderful that the children never could tire of them.

At first the children did not know how to read at all, but they loved to look at the book, and wondered what it said. After a time one child studied the book until he understood one of the most simple stories. Then he told the other children about it, and soon many of them were trying to read from the book. When they had read a few of the stories, these helped them to understand others; and the more they read, the more interested they became. Let me tell you one of the stories in this wonderful book.

Here is a green hill where children love to run and play. It looks like many another hill that you have seen; still there is something strange about it. There is an opening in its side, and people go down into the ground under the hill. Let us go in, too.

Here is an elevator for us, but it is not like the one you have seen in the stores with a carpet on the floor and cushioned seats. It is rough and dirty. We go down, down, down into the darkness. When we reach the bottom, a rough-looking man with dirty clothes comes to us to show the way. We follow him through long passages and halls with rooms on each side where we see men at work. We hear the echoes as the men pound great blocks, or as they sometimes speak to one another. All around are black walls and arches.

If we look about us, we shall see in the walls the forms of beautiful ferns or of palm-leaves. Sometimes we see something that looks like the trunk of a tree. In another place we find a tiny shell like that of some nut. Here are mosses and little leaves. Ferns and mosses, nuts, palms, and trees are all perfect in shape and beautiful in form, yet away under this hill.

Have you guessed what the story is about? Have you seen that we have been down into a coal-mine, and that these black walls are coal made by the trees and ferns ages and ages ago? Have you ever thought what we should do if we had not the coal to make our fires, to heat the rooms, and to cook our food? It is a wonderful story, is it not? But there are many more just as interesting in this book that the father has written. How many of you can tell what this wonderful book is? It is this dear old earth on which we live, and God has written it for us, his children. In it we can find the most beautiful and wonderful tales if only we learn to read them.

Let us try to see the beauty in the blue dome of the sky, with its fleecy white clouds or its beautiful stars; let us listen to the song of the birds and learn of the different flowers, so that some day we may be able to read and understand some of the more wonderful stories that our Father has written for us.

LESSON IV.

GROWTH OF PLANTS.

" Consider the lilies of the field, how they grow." — Matt. 6 : 28.

THE Bible tells us that God said, "Let the earth put forth grass, herb yielding seed, and fruit-tree bearing fruit after its kind, wherein is the seed thereof, upon the earth : and it was so."

God had made the earth ready for the plants, as we have learned ; but there was no one upon the earth to plant the seeds, to water the trees and care for the plants. God had arranged that the grass and herbs and trees should plant their own seed, find their own food, and get their own water themselves. In each plant, no matter how small it is, there is a seed which will grow into other plants just like itself. Each plant leads its own life and cares for its own children. It drops its tiny seed to the ground where it can take root and grow.

If you cut into an apple, what will you find? Yes, seeds ; and each tiny seed contains a real little apple-tree, but so small that we cannot see much shape to it. When the petals of the flower have dropped to the ground, the little green ball appears, which grows and grows until it has become the rosy-cheeked apple-filled with sugar and sunshine. God makes all his gifts work together for our good. Is it not a wonderful thing that the sweet, juicy apple can grow from the pink and white blossom ? A more wonderful thing still is the fact that God planned the beau-

GOLDEN LEAVES.
From a painting by J. E. Grace.

tiful flower and the juicy apple for you and me, for all the people on this earth.

Think how many different kinds of flowers there are, and how differently they grow, and how beautiful each one is. Can you see anything in a violet that looks like a rose? Does it seem as if the daisy and the clover could come from the same place? Yet we see them side by side in the fields. How different are the buttercup and the wild aster! Yet God made them both. He made so many, many other different kinds that you and I do not even know the names of them all.

God not only made the plants to look unlike each other, but he also planned many ways for them to grow. Did you ever notice the winged seed of the maple, and how far the wind often carries it from the tree? If the new little maple-tree were to try to grow close to the mother tree it would not have room enough or sunshine sufficient to grow into a large, strong tree. God has given the seeds these wings that they may fly away from the older tree to a place where there will be more room in which to grow, and God has planned the wind to help the seeds. There are many seeds that are carried to other places by the wind. Sometimes the seeds float down a river to some new ground, where they take root and grow. I am sure that even you boys and girls have helped some of the seeds to find new homes. How many of you have blown the dandelion seeds to watch the feathery tufts sail off so lightly through the air from the tiny, fairy-like cushion where they have rested? That was just what the seed was longing to have done; and, if you had not helped it, the wind would have come along and given it a whiff.

God has arranged many other ways for the seeds to find new places in which to grow so that the whole earth may be made beautiful. See whether you can find any other curious ways in which seeds reach their new homes.

Now let us remember that God made these beautiful plants and all the wonderful things upon the earth for us, for the men and women and little children, and that he was ages getting the earth ready for us. There are so many things on this dear old earth that God has planned for us that we are only beginning to find them. Do you think the grass and the trees, the flowers and the ferns, the quiet ponds and the sparkling brooks, the grand old hills and the mighty oceans, have made this world as beautiful as were the bubbles we made during the first lesson? But there are many, many more beauties that God has added to this earth for our sakes, and sometime we may learn about a few of them.

MEMORY GEM.

Spake full well, in language quaint and olden,
    One who dwelleth by the castled Rhine,
When he called the flowers so blue and golden,
    Stars, that in earth's firmament do shine.

Wondrous truths, and manifold as wondrous,
    God hath written in those stars above;
But not less in the bright flowerets under us
    Stands the revelation of his love.
              — *Henry W. Longfellow.*

OCCUPATION.

Show the seeds in the apple, also cut a cross section to find the form of the blossom. Give each child a different flower, having, if possible, some winged seeds among the number, and speak briefly of each variety.

STORY.— THE MILKWEED SEEDS.

There were once a dozen purplish pink blossoms on a tall, stout stem. They awoke when the glad sun smiled upon them in the morning, and closed their petals in sleep when it grew dark. After a time the petals fell off one by one. A long pod or pocket grew around what had been the blossom, and inside of this the seeds began to change. After a time there came white fleecy tufts of silk as a crown to each little brown seed, but they were still incased in the pocket. While they were hidden in the pod they talked together; they wondered whether they were always to remain there. One was discontented, and longed to fly away.

"If I can ever leave this dark house," he said, "I shall fly as far as I can and see this great world."

"But something might happen to you," said the second seed. "Would it not be better to stay where we are?"

"O, I'm not afraid!" answered the first. "I can take care of myself."

"What shall you do?" asked the third brown seed of the next one lying so close to it.

"I am sure there is some work for us to do," answered the fourth; "and I am ready to wait and see what it is."

The other seeds thought this so sensible an answer that they decided to do the same.

At length the pod burst open; and, when there came a puff of wind, the first little seed flew away. It knew not where it was going or what would become of it. As it began to go down toward the earth, not far from the brown pod, it felt sorry because it wished to see more of the world. Just at this instant, however, there came another gust of wind and whirled it far up into the air, until it was dizzy and sick. How much it wished itself safe back with the other seeds in the long pod! It saw so many strange sights that it was frightened. At last it was so tired that it hardly knew what was happening to it, and it fell into the road, and was trampled upon by a heavy wagon.

The other seeds still lay closely packed in their small house; but each day the pod opened a little wider, and, as it swayed in the wind, they found they had to cling to the inside to prevent being blown away. One day two children came along, and one of them exclaimed: "O, here is a milkweed pod! Let us each take one of the seeds for a boat to sail in a little pond we can make in one of mother's dishes." So two of the silky-tufted seeds were carried to the children's home, where they amused the little baby brother while their tired mother had a rest; and the brown seeds were glad, for they had found their work.

The next day the wind blew so hard that three seeds were carried away from the pod and blown to different places where they lay through the winter, oftentimes covered by the snow. In the spring they sent down little roots into the ground and a shoot up toward the sunlight, and after a time this shoot became a long stalk with blossoms upon it, and then there was another pod with seeds inside.

The rest of the seeds still clung to the pod, until one day a boy came skipping along and gathered them into a bag, where they found many others like themselves. When he had his bag full, he carried it home. The boy and his mother separated the little seeds from the downy tufts of silk, and put the latter into a pillow with many more like them. The pillow was for his sick sister. As she rested her head upon the soft, cool pillow, she felt very grateful to her brother for all his work in gathering the silky threads. And the tufts of silk themselves were glad because they could help some one. Even the brown seeds that were thrown away were happy, because they had held some of the silk threads that now made the pillow.

LESSON V.

THE SUN, MOON, AND STARS.

" Truly the light is sweet, and a pleasant thing it is for the eyes to behold the sun." — Eccl. 11 : 7.

"GOD said, Let there be lights in the firmament of the heaven to divide the day from the night ; and let them be for signs, and for seasons, and for days and years ; and let them be for lights in the firmament of the heaven to give light upon the earth ; and it was so."

All around the earth had been a dense cloud. After a long, long time, however, this cloud disappeared, some of it becoming water which made rivers and seas. After this cloud disappeared there were seen great lights in the sky. Do you think they looked like electric lights? No, they were very much larger. What did the Bible say they were for? "To divide the day from the night." Now you can guess what they were. The sun to light the day, and the moon and the stars to shine at night. The earth turned around each day just as it does now. So, when our side of the earth is toward the sun, it is light where we are, and we call it day; but, as our side of the earth turns away from the sun, it is dark and we call it night.

Before this there had been no summer and winter, no day and night, because the cloud prevented the sun's rays from reaching the earth. Probably it was not as cold anywhere on the earth then as it is in some parts now. The Frost King did not build beautiful ice bridges and palaces or caves and shining

THE SUN, MOON, AND STARS.   47

grottoes, or make pictures of trees and vines. He could not make the water of the pond so that you could run and skate over it as children do in the cold countries now. The north wind did not send down any feathery, white flakes of snow to cover the ground and make the fences and trees look as if they belonged to fairy-land. It was warm all over the earth all the time as it is now in some parts. But sometimes it was light and sometimes it was dark.

God planned that the sun should give us light during the day when our side of the earth is turned toward it. At night it is not as light. The moon is not so bright as the sun; it shines very faintly in the daytime because the light from the sun is so much brighter. In the night, however, it gives us a white, silvery light quite different from that of the sun.

Some of the stars are great worlds something like the one on which we live, and they get their light from the sun as we do. There are Jupiter and Mars and Venus, and several others of which you will learn when you are older. Venus is of nearly the same size as this earth. They are so far away that they look small to us.

Besides these worlds, or planets, as we call them, there are many, many more stars that are like our sun. They are a great distance away, and must be very large and bright in order to be seen from here. These stars or suns are so far away from us and from one another that it is possible that they, too, have different worlds going around them as our earth and Jupiter and Venus go around our sun.

God cares for all these stars; he keeps them moving just where they should go. Do you suppose he can stop to think of one little boy or girl on this earth, which is only one of so many worlds? The Bible says: "Are not two sparrows sold for a farthing? and not one of them shall fall on the ground without your Father [that means God]; but the very hairs of your head are all numbered. Fear not therefore; ye are of more value than many sparrows."

If God cares for each little sparrow, surely he will care for the boys and girls. God can think of all these different things at once and of a great many others besides. Do not you believe he thought of how much the children would like to watch the beautiful stars at night, when he let their light shine to be seen upon this earth? Do not you also believe he thought of the boys and girls when he planned that sometimes the moon should look full and round like a ball, and sometimes look like a crescent? God not only made all these wonderful things, but he was glad to plan them all for our enjoyment. Men have learned a great deal about the stars, as well as of many other beautiful things God has made; but no one could have learned any of these things if God had not given him a mind to study and understand them.

MEMORY GEM.

Silently, one by one, in the infinite meadows
    of heaven,
Blossomed the lovely stars, the forget-me-nots
    of the angels.
              — *Henry W. Longfellow.*

OCCUPATION.

Let the children hold objects to represent the earth, the moon, and the stars. Use a large ball for the earth, and have plainly marked upon it a spot to represent the home of the children. Use a lamp or other light for the sun. Have the lamp placed in a position so that the child who holds the ball that represents the earth can move around the lamp and its light shall properly shine upon the earth. Have the child turn the ball slowly around to illustrate our day and night. Let him also make the ball circle around the light as does our earth during the year.

Other children should be supplied with paper stars. The story that follows will be more clear if seven of the children with stars form the Dipper.

STORY.—THE LEGEND OF THE DIAMOND DIPPER.

There are a great many stories so old that no one knows who wrote them. Some of them are true and some are not. But many are so beautiful that we love them even though we do not know that they really happened. Sometimes we call these "wonder" stories, legends; sometimes we call them myths. We have been talking about the sun and the moon and the stars, and you know that seven of the stars are called "The Great Dipper."

I once heard of an old lady who was listening to a group of young people talking about the stars which they had just been out-of-doors to see. She heard them talking about the Great Dipper and the Little Dipper, and she said, "You must have better eyes than I have, for I can't see anything like a dipper in the sky; they all look like stars to me."

This dear old lady thought that by the Great Dipper was meant some one star that looked like a dipper. She did not understand that we mean seven stars so arranged that four of them form the bowl and three of them the handle of the dipper. I should like to tell you a legend, a wonder story about a dipper, because the story is so beautiful.

The story is told that in a certain country the people believed that there was a dipper covered with diamonds, which would be a great blessing to the one who found it. But no one could find this diamond dipper unless he was good and pure and unselfish. Many persons had sought for this wonderful dipper, but had not found it. Oftentimes they made presents to those about them, hoping that by being generous they should be able to find the treasure.

When a new child came into the world, the legend tells us, he was told of the diamond dipper; and many children looked for it. One day a little child had been told the story by his mother, who gave him a tin dipper that he might understand what to look for. The child was so interested in the story and so anxious to find the beautiful treasure that he started at once, carrying with him the tin dipper. He ran here and there, searching under trees and behind rocks, and wherever he thought it might be found. At length he grew very tired, and lay down to rest. When he awoke, he again looked for the wonderful dipper, but he had been searching so long that he had become hungry and faint; he was also very thirsty.

He wandered about, trying to find some water to quench his thirst; but he had gone so far from his own home that he had come to a place where there was none, and every one was suffering for the want of it. As the child walked on, he thought, "If I could but have my dipper filled with cool water, how glad I should be, even if I could not find the diamond dipper!" Then he prayed; and, as he looked at his dipper, he saw that it was full of clear water. The child also saw a little harebell with hanging head and wilted stalk, bending down to the ground for want of water. Then the child knelt and carefully sprinkled the water over the thirsty plant. He was so much interested in having the water go where it would most help the flower that he did not see that his dipper still held as much water as before, or that it was no longer a tin dipper, but that it had been changed to silver.

The child arose and was about to drink some of the precious water himself, when a dog fell panting at his side. The child could not bear to see the suffering of the dog, and quickly poured some of the water into the palm of his hand, and stooped for the dog to drink. Near by was the harebell, which now stood up straight and strong because of the child's unselfish act. As the child gave some of the water to the thirsty dog, the happy harebell rung some of its silver notes and softly sung, for it knew that the dipper had been changed from silver to gold.

Again the child arose to drink from the dipper some of the refreshing water, for he was very thirsty, when he saw a poor man standing at his side, who begged for a little water to quench his thirst. The child lifted the dipper to the man, and gave to him before he had so much as tasted the precious water himself. As the man drank, there came a wonderful light and a voice which said, "Inasmuch as ye did it unto one of these my brethren, even these least, ye did it unto me." As the child looked into the shining eyes of the man, he seemed to see the beautiful Christ standing before him, and then he was gone. The child stood looking at the spot where the lovely form had been, and then turned away with a happy feeling in his own heart. As he wandered on, having forgotten his own thirst because of the joy of having helped another, he lifted the dipper and saw that it was covered with flashing diamonds. His own unselfish acts had changed the common tin dipper into one of diamonds.

LESSON VI.

CORAL.

" The works of the Lord are great." — Ps. III: 2.

LONG ago, way back at the time when the earth appeared so different from the way it looks now, down in the sea was a little hill of mud and sand all covered with water. Not far from it floated some soft jelly-like animals. After a little time each one fastened himself to a bit of rock near this hill. Here he stayed, eating all the time with a tiny mouth, drinking in the sea-water.

In the water were little particles of a white limestone substance which the polyp drew into its mouth with the water, and used it to build up around its body a sort of limestone house. This helped to protect the little polyp from the fishes in the ocean, for they do not care to eat a hard piece of shell. Yes, it is really a kind of shell house that the little polyp has built about him. But the little animal never leaves the house; he always stays inside. Most of you have found the shells of oysters and snails along the seashore. These animals made their shells in something the same way as the polyp.

But let us go back to Coraltown, where a great many coral polyps had fastened themselves to the rock and had built their houses; after a time it became a village of polyps. Other coral polyps fastened themselves to the houses of the first animals, and built their castles. Fastened to these were still more polyps, and so on, until after years and years the little hill of mud that was first there became surrounded by these tiny little houses of father and mother, brother and sister polyps, side by side and above each other, forming a circle around the hill. Still there were more and more of the polyps, and the pile of houses grew higher and higher as years and years went by, until at last the topmost houses were almost at the top of the water.

When storms came, bits of the tiny walls were broken off. The polyps had worked for years and years building the walls, and these were often broken in a moment; but God had planned it all, and had a wonderful purpose in thus letting the waves break down their houses. These crumbling bits that broke off floated about and filled the little holes in the wall. The rough edges at the top caught seaweed and bits of wood drifting about, and sometimes dirt and sand. When the top of this circle, made by the little animals, was above the water, the winds blowing across the ocean from the land often left seeds of plants upon the dirt on the top of the coral rock. The birds also brought seeds and dropped in the cracks. These soon became plants, and grew until the place looked like a little island with green plants and shrubs growing upon it, and a beautiful quiet lake inside. Do you suppose the coral polyps would have known their old homes? We must remember, however, that it took thousands and thousands of years for the tiny animals to build this up so high.

I am sure you all think it wonderful that such mites of bodies could do so great a work, and also that they should know how to make these walls for themselves. If they could have thought, they would certainly have thanked the heavenly Father for putting plenty of the white limestone substance into the water, where they could so readily get it to use for building up their bodies.

Now remember that many other animals besides

the coral polyps also use this same thing for their shells. Another thing I should like to tell you about it. You also build it into your body, into the bones of these hands and arms. They would soon grow weak and useless without it. You do not know how you do it, but God has so arranged it that your body does it without your realizing it. You could not toss a ball or run and jump if your bones had not thus been made strong and hard. We, as well as the sea-animals, should thank the heavenly Father.

MEMORY GEM.

All things bright and beautiful,
 All creatures great and small,
All things wise and wonderful,—
 The Lord God made them all.
　　　　　　　　　　　—John Keble.

OCCUPATION.

Show the children different specimens of corals. Show as many varieties as possible, and explain to them by means of each specimen. Draw a picture of a living polyp with its waving branches. Then let the children draw or cut out pictures of as many different sea-animals as there is time for, not omitting the shell-fish. This work must be prepared beforehand by collecting pictures of the different fishes and other forms of sea life for the children to copy.

STORY.—THE THREE TROUT.

A pretty little stream ran through a meadow where daisies and buttercups grew. This cool brook was the home of three little fishes, whose names were Tommy Trout, Jacky Trout, and Dicky Trout. Happy little fishes they were. A good fairy watched over them, and they had everything that a trout could wish for. They darted about among the reeds, and chased each other round and round the stones. In the warm, sunny days you might have seen them leaping far out of the water to catch the flies. Sometimes they would lie quite still for a minute, and listen to the lowing of the cows. Then off again, darting to and fro, and sporting about in the cool stream.

But, as time went on, and these trout grew older and bigger, two of them, Tommy and Jacky, became sad and unhappy. All their merry play was gone, and now for hours together they would lie quite still under the bank.

The good fairy was very sorry to see this change in her little friends, and one day called them to her.

"Why are you so sad?" she asked. "Have I not given you all that a trout can wish? Tell me what I can do to bring back your cheerful looks, and make you merry and happy again. You, Tommy, may speak first, as you are the eldest. Tell me what I can do to please you."

Now Tommy had grown up to be a very proud little trout. He had become unhappy because other trout were as good as himself. He wished to be above them all. So he said: "Give me wings, good fairy. Make me like the lark that flies away up in the blue sky."

No sooner had he spoken than his tiny fins grew into strong, broad wings. Then he rose out of the water, and flew up into the air. Away he went over the trees and the hills, and far up among the thin white clouds.

"Now," he said, "I am far above those poor little trout that are swimming about in their little brook. That may be good enough for them, but this is the life for me."

And Tommy Trout flew on and on until he had gone many miles from his old home. At last he felt hungry and tired, and wished to go back for a while to the stream where he had left Jacky and Dicky. So down he flew toward the earth. But alas! he had lost his way. He fell not into the cool brook, but among hard rocks and dry, hot sand. He could not find a drop of water to drink. Up again he mounted to the air, but a second time he fell among the same hard rocks and dry, hot sand. Up and down and up and down he flew, trying in vain to reach the stream where he had once been so happy. He was at last so tired out that he was not able to rise at all, but lay gasping among the stones.

Jacky Trout was not so proud as Tommy; but he, too, had faults. He did not care what became of the others if only he himself was safe and snug. So, when the fairy asked him what he would like, he said: "I have heard of poor trout being caught by men, and carried off in baskets. Teach me, kind fairy, all their tricks to catch us, that I may know how to keep myself from harm."

Then the fairy told him all about the net, of which he was so much afraid. It is sometimes drawn through the water, and so shuts in the fishes that few ever get out of it. Then she told of the cruel hook with its sharp point. She told how men cover it with bait to make little fishes think it is only a fly or a worm.

"Thank you, good fairy," said Jacky. And off he went, thinking himself happier than all the other trout.

In the warm days of summer, Dicky would often jump out after a big, fat fly. Poor Jacky was always in great fear, lest he should be caught by a hook. He often said: "Foolish Dick! Why, it may not be a fly at all, but only a sharp hook." When a cloud passed over the brook and cast its shadow on the water, Jacky was sure it was a net.

And thus selfish Jacky always lived in a state of fear. As he was never at peace, he was never happy. He was afraid to eat his dinner lest a hook might be in it. So he grew thinner and thinner.

"What would you like?" said the kind fairy to Dicky.

Now Dicky was a good little trout. He was happy then, as he had been when the fairy first placed him in the brook. So he said: "I thank you, good fairy, for giving me this quiet, pretty stream. I have everything here to make me happy. I am always sure of a worm for dinner; and, when there are plenty of flies, I can catch some of them for supper. I wish for nothing more; so do with me as you think right. Let me do what you think is best for me."

This pleased the fairy very much, and she took great care of happy little Dicky. For a time he felt sad at the loss of Tommy and Jacky, and often thought of the happy days they had spent together. But by and by the good fairy sent other little trout to live in the same stream with Dicky, and he soon made friends with them, and the old games were played again, and Dicky was the happiest little trout that ever was seen.

LESSON VII.

ANIMAL LIFE.

"He giveth to the beast his food, and to the young ravens which cry."
— Ps. 147:9.

THINK of this world where everything was so quiet, where there was no sound except the ripple and splash of the water as it fell over the rocks of some waterfall, or as it swept back and forth on the beach in ocean waves, or the wind as it sighed through the tops of the pine-trees. Such a world would seem to us very strange with no song of birds, no lowing cattle, no sheep to say "Baa, baa." But stranger still, no human voice was anywhere heard.

At length, however, God was ready. For the Bible tells us: "God said, Let the earth bring forth the living creature after its kind, cattle, and creeping thing, and beast of the earth after its kind: and it was so. And God saw that it was good." He had the world all ready for each different kind of animal. Would you not like to have been there, to have heard the first bird's song, to have seen the first squirrel frisk up a tree, to have watched a butterfly flit from flower to flower, and to have looked into the eyes of the gentle fawn as it sped over the soft carpet of green?

Many of the animals were such as we have never seen, for the animals changed as time went on. Immense wild beasts such as the mastodon roamed the earth. Other smaller creatures, unlike any now living, dwelt in the forests.

I want to tell you of another of the wonderful

things that God did. What would all the animals do on the earth with no one to care for them? God taught each little animal how to look out for itself, how to get its own food, how to defend itself from other animals, how to protect its young. Did you ever watch a bird build its nest? Could you build such a nest as does the beautiful oriole? See how lightly and easily it swings in the wind like a cradle; yet it is so firmly built that even the winter storms do not tear it from the drooping branch of the tree where the little birds so carefully hung it the previous summer. You have hands with which to work; the bird has only its feet and beak; yet see how cleverly she builds her nest. We could not do anything like it.

Do you think all the birds build the same kind of nests? No, indeed. God has taught the crow to build a very rough nest, made of any coarse material plastered with mud, which looks very different from the oriole's soft swinging home. The woodpecker makes a hole in a dead tree for its nest; the quail scoops out a little hollow in the ground, thus making a place where its eggs may lie without rolling away; while some birds build their nests in sandy banks.

God has shown the robin how to hop along the ground and pull out the worms. He has taught the sea-gull to dive down into the water and bring up a little fish. The blue jay picks the insects off the trees as easily as we pick up and eat a piece of bread.

Not only has God given the birds this ability to take care of themselves, but he has not forgotten the other animals. The deer has very quick hearing, and is so fleet of foot that it can flee away from its enemies; the squirrel gets ready for the winter by storing up fruit and nuts; the gopher keeps from sight in its underground passages, where it can feed upon the roots of plants and trees. Many of the smaller animals are not easily seen, as they are colored very much like the ground or the trees where they are most often found.

Did you ever notice the spider's web with its fine threads woven so regularly and so securely fastened? It must be a wonderful being who could teach the tiny spider to make this strong but fine web. Think, too, of the beautiful silk that the silkworm weaves. How is it possible for so small an animal to make so lovely fine silk and so much of it? Only God could teach him.

There are thousands of just such curious and wonderful things that we could see going on all about us if only we opened our eyes to see them. These are not hidden away in God's storehouses, but are placed right before us for our enjoyment and to teach us of God's wonderful power. Perhaps sometime we can talk again of the curious and interesting things the dear Father has taught the creatures he has put on this earth.

MEMORY GEM.

Then the little Hiawatha
Learned of every bird its language;
Learned their names and all their secrets,
How they built their nests in summer,
Where they hid themselves in winter;
Talked with them whene'er he met them;
Called them "Hiawatha's chickens."
Of all beasts he learned the language,
Learned their names and all their secrets,
How the beavers built their lodges,
Where the squirrels hid their acorns,
How the reindeer ran so swiftly,
Why the rabbit was so timid;
Talked with them whene'er he met them;
Called them "Hiawatha's brothers."
— *Henry W. Longfellow.*

OCCUPATION.

Pictures of curious animals will help to illustrate this lesson. Different kinds of birds' nests will add to the interest. Bits of straw and twine, horsehair, and ravellings of worsted can be given to the children that they may try to weave a nest like some one of the birds' nests shown.

STORY.— A MONGREL'S MEMORIES.

"I am a white-haired dog, and people call me Princey. I used to be very merry, and would jump and snap at everything I saw just for sheer joy. What fun it was to run after horses and bark at their heels! *They* did n't seem to think so, and would sometimes try to send me off with their hind legs; but, whenever I met a horse so rude as that, I was offended, and would n't play any more. But now things are changed; for I am getting old and fat, and I do n't seem to like to exert myself as much as I did; a comfortable mat or a cosey window-seat, where I can see all the other little dogs running about, suits me better. My life has been a happy one as a whole. The beginning was n't very nice. I was uglier than all my brother puppies, and that was unpleasant.

"At last I was given away to a little schoolboy. He never had a dog of his own before; so he thought a great deal of me, and cuddled me up in his arms, and said the nicest things to me. He never forgot to feed me but once, and then he was so sorry about it that he gave me a splendid dinner and begged my pardon in the most polite manner, which I thought was very handsome of him, for people usually forget that we dogs have any feelings with regard to being treated politely.

"I had n't been used to such kind treatment, so I

didn't know how to show my gratitude. I began licking his face, but he didn't seem to like that much, and put me down; but I loved him, and always have loved that little boy all my life.

"He took me to his house and showed me to his brothers and sisters. Some of them liked me and some didn't. 'Ugly little mongrel,' one said. But 'my little boy,' as I've always called him, stood up for me, and I was allowed to stay. I had a hard job to make them like me. I would run and fetch things to please them, and soon learned to beg and hold the sugar on my nose without letting it drop. The brother who had called me an 'ugly little mongrel' taught me that.

"'My little boy' was always my chief friend. He and I understood each other; for a wag of my tail meant more to him than half a dozen barks would tell other people.

"And now I am thinking about that eventful day in my life when I, the 'ugly little mongrel,' showed 'my little boy' how I loved him.

"We had been in the habit of going to school together. I mean he went to school, and I went to the gate of the playground with him, where he always bade me good-by.

"Well, that day we had been so happy going through the lanes, he whistling and skipping as we went along, and I running and barking by his side, when all at once — I never understood the reason — he tripped and fell. I was in front at the time; but I soon ran back, and there he lay so white and still! To this day I can scarcely think of it without a sniff. I was so excited that I did not know what to do. I ran a wee bit; then I ran back again, licked his face and hands, and was nearly heartbroken, when he suddenly opened his eyes, looked as if he didn't know poor Princey for a minute, and then said, 'O, I remember; I fell, didn't I? And you have waited beside me, have you? Good old doggie.' I whined and wagged my tail, as if I would have left him!

"Then he tried to get up, but couldn't, as his foot seemed to double up so; then he tried to crawl along on his hands and knees; but after a minute or two I heard him say, 'It's no use; I can't keep on'; and he sunk back on the ground. 'Now, Princey,' he said, turning to me, 'I wonder if you will understand.' I pricked up my ears to try my utmost. 'You must go home. I'm sure I've either sprained my ankle very badly or broken it, and you must bring help.'

"I whined again, and licked his hands, for I knew what he meant, and was determined to do it.

"'But here,' he said, 'I'd better make sure.' With that he took off his necktie. 'Now, my brave dog, away home and bring help.'

"I needed no more, and away I ran as I never ran before.

"On reaching home, I tore up the stairs, rushed into the sitting-room, and caught hold of the servant's dress with my teeth.

"'Bless the puppy, what's the matter with him?' But I only barked and tugged the more.

"'Look here, children,' she called out, 'there's something wrong with this puppy; just look at him.'

"They all came around me, and I ran first to one and then to another, jumping to each of them, till at last one said, 'Why, he has Archie's tie around his neck.'

"I barked louder at this, and ran to the door. They followed me, and I still ran on. 'Let's see what he means,' I was glad to hear them say; and they came on after me, and I led them to where 'my little boy' lay. He was lying quite still and moaning painfully, but he was glad to see his brothers and sisters.

"Well, after some little time he was carried home, and I did n't see him for hours; but the rest of the children were so kind to me. 'Was n't it clever of Princey?' said one. 'He's just a dear little doggie,' said another.

"At last I saw my 'dear little boy'; he had asked for me, and I was taken to see him. What we said to each other I cannot exactly remember, we were both so much moved; but I know it sealed a lifelong friendship. And now years have passed since that day; and, though he is grown up, and I am no longer a puppy, it is still *his* footsteps that I listen for, *his* voice I hunger for; and *his* 'There, there, good old Princey,' seems to realize my idea of happiness."

PEACE BE TO THIS HOUSE.
From a painting by Dobson.

LESSON VIII.

MAN.

"Behold the birds of the heaven; your heavenly Father feedeth them. Are not ye of much more value than they?" — Matt. 6 : 26.

CAN you think of the world as God looked upon it so many ages ago, before there were any people here? It was covered with beautiful green, — the great trees, the shrubs and plants, the grass and flowers. Do you remember the verse we had from the Bible, "Consider the lilies of the field, how they grow; they toil not, neither do they spin: yet I say unto you, that even Solomon in all his glory was not arrayed like one of these"? Where did the lilies and the other flowers get their beauty? Then there was the ocean, with its changing blue and green and gray. Beautiful brooks flowed peacefully along by wooded shores, and grew into broad rivers, or became cataracts falling over the rocks. The waters were thronged with fishes and all the various sea-animals; the land was covered with creatures of many kinds; and the air was filled with birds and insects. At night the bright stars and the shining moon gave light to the earth.

God was pleased with the world which he had made, but one thing more was necessary before his work was finished. "God said, Let us make man in our image, after our likeness: and let them have dominion over the fish of the sea, and over the fowl of the air, and over the cattle, and over all the earth, and over every creeping thing that creepeth upon the earth."

God planned the world for the needs of all the animals; everything they could care for was on the earth ready for them, but the world was not made for them alone. The world and all there is upon it God made for men, women, and children, for their enjoyment and for their good. He made man very different from any of the other animals. Some of the animals know more and can understand more than others. Some of them can remember; others have no memory. Dogs often show great fondness for their masters; pigs do not seem to know any difference between those that daily give them food and those that do not. But God gave to people much more than to any animal. He gave them greater knowledge and understanding. They have minds, and the power to care for and use more of the good things about them. God has given us power over the animals, and he expects us to care for them and be kind to them. He has taught us how to use the animals; how to train the elephant to carry heavy loads, the horse to draw the carriage, and the dog to protect the house and its people.

We can think, we can study, we can learn, we can teach others. But God has given us much more than this. We have something that no animal has at all. After a time the dog and the cat, the horse and the cow, can no longer run about. They are dead, and that is the end of them. They have no longer any life. But God has given to people souls that will always live. God will live forever. There will always be God. We, too, shall live forever. In that God has made us like himself. We have not always lived as he has. There was a time when there were no you and I, when there were no people at all. You know we have been talking about it. We have not all power as God has. You know he can do anything. But he has given us souls that shall live forever; so he wishes us to try to live good, pure lives like his, to do what is right, to be kind and loving and unselfish, that we may live with him forever.

God watches over us all the time, and is always ready to help us do what is right; he is always near us to care for us, that no harm may come to us; he loves us because we are his children.

MEMORY GEM.

God's in his heaven,
All's right with the world.
— *Robert Browning.*

OCCUPATION.

With the sand-box and grass, twigs, flowers, and moss make a portion of the earth. On this place different animals (if nothing better is at hand, cut pictures from some paper), and among them two or three men. Let the men use the oxen to plough, or the carrier pigeon to carry some message, being careful to have them always thoughtful and kind to the animals.

The principal point to bring out in this lesson is the fact that God has given to man an imperishable soul. Make it easy for the children to understand.

STORY.— PHILLY'S FAIRIES.

Once upon a time there was a poor little boy who did not live at home, but had to work for his clothes and what he had to eat. Most of the time he was good, and kept still when the people for whom he worked were cross, and would not be satisfied, no matter what he did to please them.

One hot day, Philly had been running errands until it was almost dark; then he ran out in the twilight, — that is always the fairies' best time, you know, — and he threw himself on the grass under a great green apple-tree.

He began wondering whether there were ever going to be bright, nice things for him such as some boys had, when all at once there was the most beautiful little object right in the middle of that apple-tree. She was swinging on a twig, and her dress was all lace, and her face was white and sweet.

Then Philly looked, and there in the sky was such a rainbow! Pink and blue and yellow and green, all in stripes. All in and out of the rainbow were tiny little specks of fairies. They had wings no bigger than a butterfly's; and they danced on nothing; and their yellow, golden hair was like crowns all around their dear little faces. They did not look at Philly lying there so still, with his eyes shut, under the green apple-tree; but he could see that they were watching the lovely fairy in the tree, and then poor Philly saw that the queen fairy was looking right at him. It set him trembling, for her eyes were not like any eyes he had ever seen before. Soon he felt better; he forgot his hard work, and begun to wonder whether such a little beauty did not have a sweet voice, and whether she would speak to him.

Just then the little angel said: "Yes, I know all about it, poor little Philly. All about the hard work, and all the long errands, and the tiredness way inside your little jacket where your heart's beating. But I have something that will help you. It will make you forget the hard work and the tired aches." Then she shook her fairy wand, and cried, "Come, little Patience; go shake your fairy dew over Philly, and help him to be like you."

And one of the beautiful fairies, with eyes just as blue as the sky, came and shook some little pink and gold shells over Philly. It made him feel better and stronger, and he began to wonder what had made him think it was so hard to do right, and he felt as if some one cared for him. Poor little Philly, who worked so hard all day!

Then the fairy in the apple-tree called again, "Come, little Forgive; take your fairy harp and go and sing to Philly one of your sweet songs."

And the rainbow swung in the sky, and down flew a cunning little fairy with a harp full of the finest strings, and she sung and sung, and the tears ran down Philly's face; but they were glad tears, and he wanted to forgive folks for being cross and hard, and never thinking to say, "Thank you."

Then again the fairy called, "Come, little Love; go throw your elfin sparks over this Philly boy, and let him taste the most beautiful thing there ever was; and that is love."

The rainbow threw out fresh streaks of red and pink and yellow and green; and a shining creature came flying along; and all the air grew full of roses and lilies and other sweet flowers; and she flew to and fro right over Philly's head; and the rainbow sparks came dropping, dropping like cool showers over his face until he felt all covered over with love. And the angel in the apple-tree cried: "Now you know there's some one loves and watches you, Philly. I can't speak the name, because it's holy. But this Love is everywhere, and all the boys and girls and little children are under its beautiful colors. It loves them forever and ever, even when they are cross and naughty; and, if they only let them, all its little spirits, Patience and Forgive and all the rest, would come and help them. There are always lovely spirits in the air, Philly, and they really want to be the children's friends, and they want to be the friends of everybody."

Then all the fairy angels spread their little webby wings and faded into the air, and the rainbow got further and further, and melted softly away, and Philly opened his eyes. He tried to remember what he had seen; but he could not, only that some one had come and talked to him about loving him. Then he said to himself, dreamy-like, "There's certainly been some one trying to make me feel better, and I want to be a real good boy." — *Adapted from "Little Jolliby's Christmas," by Harriet A. Cheever. Congregational Publishing Society.*

LESSON IX.

CONTENTMENT.

"God saw that it was good." — *Gen. 1 : 25.*

The Bible, after telling how God made the earth and the plants and the animals, says, "God saw that it was good." After he had made man the Bible says again, "God saw everything that he had made, and, behold, it was very good."

God gives us our homes, our fathers and mothers, our friends, our pleasures, our playthings, our food. Whatever we have comes from God, and he sees that it is all good for us. We may not have so fine a house or so many toys as some other child whom we know; but we have what God gives us, we have just what God sees is best for us, and therefore it is "good." As God sees that it is good for us, so we also should feel that it is good.

Instead of fussing because we have not a doll as large as Helen's, or a top that sings when it spins like Frank's, we should be glad that we have any doll or any top. How kind God has been to give us toys! Let us try to be glad and happy with whatever we have. If we share our playthings with others, we shall make them happy and ourselves also. If we smile and are good-natured all the time, we shall be a little like God, for we thus show that we also think that what he gives is good.

Very often it is cloudy or it rains, and then we cannot see the sun; but, if there is a little boy or girl with a sunny face, one that is happy and glad all day long, it is like having sunshine in the house. If, when papa comes down to breakfast, he sees his little boy with a bright and happy face, he will remember it all day long, and it will help him. If the dear sunny girl does not complain because it rains and keeps her in the house, and is happy with her playthings, then her round little face seems like the merry sun itself. She therefore helps to make big brother and sister happier and better through the day because she thinks that whatever God sends is good.

But there is some one else, whom the bright little face helps the most of any one, and that is mamma. How great a help it is to her, when she is busy and perhaps tired, to have her little boy play happily with what playthings he has, and not tease for others or wish that he had something new, a drum or a train of cars!

If Myra frets because she has no doll-carriage as Edith has, it makes mamma feel bad; but, if Myra plays with her dolly with a happy face, and thinks that a box that she can pull with a string will do just as well to take her doll to ride in, then mamma is happy and Myra is pleasing God.

When boys and girls are happy with what God has given them, and do not wish for what they have not, they not only please God, but they are really helping him. Think of it. It is a wonderful thing that God has arranged that we can really help him. We love to help father and mother, and feel that we are pretty big when we can really help mamma, but how much more it is to be able to help God! Little boys and little girls can help God carry out his great plan, and it is a part of this same beautiful plan that all his children shall be happy and contented all the time.

So, when little boys or girls are sunny and pleasant all day, then they are mamma's sunshines. If we learn to be happy and contented when children, we shall grow up to be cheerful men and women. Suppose we try to be little sunshines each day.

MEMORY GEM.

> I know not where his islands lift
>   Their fronded palms in air;
> I only know I cannot drift
>   Beyond his love and care.
> —*John G. Whittier.*

OCCUPATION.

Provide several sheets of stiff paper, mucilage, pencils, scissors, and some blocks.

Ask each child to think of something that he would like to have to play with the next week, and then see whether he cannot make with the blocks or cut from the paper something that will take the place of the desired article. If he cannot do this for himself, help him a little by suggestions. If the teacher can think of no way to make the particular object, lead the child's mind to something else. Tell him that perhaps God wishes him to do without that particular toy and to be satisfied with something else. If possible, however, the teacher should help the child carry out his original plan. Let the teacher think beforehand how to make as many different kinds of toys as possible.

To make a rocking-horse, draw and cut from the paper two horses, and fasten them together by a strip of paper gummed to each horse. On top of this can be placed a paper boy.

For a doll's rocking-chair a little practice beforehand will enable the teacher to help the child draw a shape that when cut out will fold to form a rocking-chair.

STORY.—SUPPOSE.

"Now you will have the whole morning for play," said the two mammas, as they went into the house, leaving the little cousins alone on the doorstep of the old farmhouse kitchen.

"What shall we do first?" said Phœbe, who lived on the farm, while Kittie was only making her a visit. "What do you like to play best?"

"I do n't know," said Kittie; "I like lawn-tennis very well. We often have lots of fun at home on the sidewalk with our roller skates; and, O, 'authors.' Do n't you like that?"

"What is it?" and Kittie described the game.

"But I have no games," said Phœbe. "I used to have a croquet set once, but some of the balls are lost, and I do n't know where to find the wickets. They are all broken, anyhow."

"Have you a lawn-tennis court?"

"No, but I saw one once." Phœbe was beginning to feel bad.

"Well, what do you play, then?" said Kittie, who was quite ready for any new fun.

"O!" cried Phœbe, brightening at once, "I play 'suppose.'"

"What — is — that?" said Kittie.

"Why, pretend, you know. We can begin now. Let us climb up on the wood-pile and pretend we are two little girls!"

"But we 're that now," said Kittie.

"O, well, never mind; we can pretend we 're not," called out Phœbe, who was already scrambling up the wood-pile. "Let 's play suppose this was a desert island, and we were two shipwrecked sailors. No, I 'll be the sailor, because I know the place better; and you can be a lady, and I 'll do everything to rescue you and your child."

"I wish I had my doll," said Kittie.

"Never mind about the doll," said Phœbe. "Here, let us pretend this was your child," and she thrust into the astonished Kittie's arms a small, round log. "Ah, ma'am, how sorry I am for your troubles! But let me lead you to a place of safety. Sit down and rest on this moss. (Pretend this log is moss.) Here is a place for your precious baby. I'll go and catch some fish, and you must be fixing things at home. Get some chips together, and surprise me with a fire when I come back. Play suppose I was your husband. Don't be anxious, dear; I'll come back with food for you and our child. I'm going to fish. I'll climb down and pick up some apples. We can play they are roots that are good to eat."

"Well," said Kittie, a little puzzled by Phœbe's lively "supposes," but beginning to think it great fun, "I'll dress the child in my apron; and, when we've had the apples, I'll go with you and explore."

"O, yes!" exclaimed Phœbe, "We will cross to the barn on the top of the stone wall, and pretend the hens are wild beasts. I hear one of them growling now; she must have laid an egg."

All the long summer days the two little girls played in the shadow of the great barn or by the haymows or the old stone wall. It was all a new world to Kittie, and was there ever such a playmate as Phœbe? She was never at a loss. Did the sun shine too hotly on the little heads, making Kittie impatient to reach the shade in the meadows beyond, Phœbe was ready with: "Let us play suppose we were riding on camels in the desert. Put your handkerchief on your head for a turban, Kittie, and take care your camel does not kneel down." And how short the way became!

Were they sent to the village on an errand, then

at once they became an army, marching to attack the town with banners of goldenrod and muskets of mullein-stalks, or they were two yellow butterflies, bound to touch every purple thistle-top they passed on their way.

Some of the very happiest days were the ones when Phœbe played suppose that Kittie was a queen, dressed in a white window-curtain, with a truly elegant crown made of dried apples around her head; and she was, by turns, her dressing-maid, her prancing steed, or one of her loyal subjects. Then suddenly the two little girls would become two brown mice, and scamper from the attic to the pantry and back again, with cookies and bits of cheese in their hands.

All too quickly the summer days passed, and Kittie was on her way to her city home again.

"You will miss Phœbe, shall you not?" said her mother, as they were sitting together in the parlor car. "What will you do without her?"

"I don't know," said Kittie, thoughtfully. "Do you know, mamma, I have ever so many more things at home than she has; but Phœbe never seems to need them, because she can have everything — don't you see? — as long as she can play 'suppose.'" —*Gertrude Linnell.*

LESSON X.

THE SEVENTH DAY.

"Remember the Sabbath day, to keep it holy." — *Exod. 20 : 8.*

WHEN God had finished making the earth, when the grass and trees had grown, when the fishes and animals had been made, and when even man was here on the earth, then God rested from his work. The Bible says, "The heavens and the earth were finished, and all the host of them." God ended his work which he had made, and he rested from all his work, and God blessèd the day and hallowed it.

After a time, when there were a great many people on the earth, God gave them ten commandments, which taught what he wanted them to do. One of the commandments was this: "Remember the Sabbath day, to keep it holy. Six days shalt thou labor, and do all thy work: but the seventh day is a sabbath unto the Lord thy God: in it thou shalt not do any work, thou, nor thy son, nor thy daughter, thy man servant, nor thy maid servant, nor thy cattle, nor the stranger that is within thy gates." Then it tells how the Lord made heaven and earth, the sea and animals, and then rested; "wherefore the Lord blessed the Sabbath day, and hallowed it."

How beautiful a thing it is that God gave us one day in seven to rest from our work, to be God's day; and he blessed it! In the commandment it says we shall do no work; that means no unnecessary work. We must eat each day, that we may live. The animals, too, must be fed. God would not wish to have the animals suffer. We should feed them and care for them, but not make them work when there is no need of it.

We ought to do on God's day what will please him. We are so busy during the week that we often have but little time to read his book, or to think of all that he has done for us. So Sunday is given to us in which to stop and enjoy his beautiful world. How pleasant it is on Sunday morning to hear the church bells ringing, calling all the people, young and old, to come to God's house, to the church that men have built in which to worship him! They invite us to come and praise God, to offer thanks for his loving care, and to listen to his word.

The Sunday school is ours also, where we can go to learn about God, and to try to understand his word and sing his praise. How could we have any of these pleasant things if God had not given us Sunday for a day of rest?

When Jesus came on the earth, he greatly enjoyed the Sabbath day. He loved to go and spend the day with his dear friends, Martha and Mary and Lazarus. You know Jesus had no home, no house of his own to live in. If he had had, do you not believe that in that home the Sabbath would have been a beautiful day? I think he would have made it the most pleasant day of all the week; not a day to run and jump and hollo in, but one in which all was quiet and peaceful, in which we could sing and talk of God. I feel sure he would have made the day so delightful that, if we were there with him, we should be very glad when the Sabbath came. We should have looked forward to that day all the week. I think that, if we had been with Jesus then, we should have had smiling faces all the time, we should have been kind and loving so as never to spoil his beautiful Sabbath.

Can we not now have just as pleasant a Sabbath as he would have had? We can, if we try.

MEMORY GEM.

> He goes on Sunday to the church,
>   And sits among his boys;
> He hears the parson pray and preach;
>   He hears his daughter's voice
> Singing in the village choir,
>   And it makes his heart rejoice.
>   — *Henry W. Longfellow.*

OCCUPATION.

Build with the blocks a church, impressing the thought that every part should be perfect and beautiful, — that which does not show, as well as the parts that are seen, — because it is God's house.

STORY. — CARL'S SUNDAY.

Ding, dong, dell! ding, dong, dell!

"Listen to the church bells!" said the sweet-faced lady Carl was learning to call Aunt Mary. "Listen! Ding, dong, dell! How pretty!"

Carl ran to the window, threw back his golden head, and listened. "It's like talking," he said. "But what are they saying? Perhaps they want me to come to church."

"Ding, dong, dell! ding, dong, dell!" said the bells, louder than ever. "Come, Carl, come! Come, Carl, come!"

"Would you like to go with us this morning, Carl? We all go to church each Sunday morning. It would not seem like Sunday to us if we did not go to church," said Aunt Mary.

As Carl sat with his aunt and cousins in the old-fashioned country church, he thought how different it was from Sunday at his own home. His father worked late Saturday night; so he was tired Sunday morning, and did not go to church. Carl must be quiet so as not to disturb him. Indeed, Sunday was a very dismal day for little Carl when at home. Even the church bells sounded different from those he heard this Sunday morning when his Aunt Mary had softly quoted " Ding, dong, dell "; for then he was not going to church.

Carl kept thinking about the bells and how they had sounded; he did not know that he ought to listen to the sermon. As he tried to remember just how they sounded, he thought it was something like this, " Listen, listen, listen." So Carl began to listen to what the minister was saying.

"Remember the Sabbath day to keep it holy. How can we keep it holy? How can these little children keep God's day holy? First, by always remembering that it is God's day, by trying to do just what they know will please him, by learning more of him." Then Carl began to wonder whether he had ever tried to please God on this day.

When church was through, Carl went with his cousin Alice into the Sunday school. He had never been to Sunday school, and had so good a time singing the motion songs and hearing the other children repeat the Bible verses! But the best of all was when they came to the lesson, and the teacher showed them a bunch of grapes with some grape leaves, and also some thorns, and told them how Jesus said that the sweet, juicy grapes cannot grow on thorn-bushes; that, if we wish to be loved, we must be loving and kind, we must bear good fruit as does the grape-vine, and not be like the thorn that pricks.

When they reached home again, they had dinner,

and each one of the children had something to eat that he liked especially; and Carl saw that his aunt had even found out what he cared most for, and had set it beside his plate. After dinner he and Alice put the Bible puzzles together, while the older children cut out and pasted into their Sunday books such pretty pictures as they could find a Bible verse for, which they wrote under the picture.

The afternoon was gone too soon for Carl, who was having so good a time that he hated to stop; but he remembered just in time about pleasing God. After supper the children all gathered around Aunt Mary's chair, while she told them one of the beautiful Bible stories, and had a quiet little talk with them. Next the children recited their verses, for each had selected and learned one for that day. When it came Carl's turn, his Aunt Mary asked him whether he would like a verse also.

"O auntie, may I have the one about 'Remember the Sabbath day to keep it holy'? I think that is such a lovely one."

"Certainly, you may have that one;" and his aunt took him up on her knee, and told the other children to go up to bed, and she would come soon. When they were gone and all was quiet, she said, "Has it been a pleasant day, Carl?"

"Yes, Aunt Mary, the best time I ever had. I never liked Sunday at home. Is it because it is all so quiet here, auntie? I never thought much about going to church before; but now I shall want to go when I hear the bells calling, 'Come, come, come.'"

"It is because we have all tried to do what will please God on his day that we have found the day such a pleasant one. Listen; there are the church bells again for evening service, 'Ding, dong, dell, Carl, good Carl.'"

After a few minutes, in which both Carl and

auntie were still, she said: "Hark! Only one bell is ringing now — 'Dong, dong, dong. Come, come, come'; and where do you think, Carl?"

"To bed, I suppose. Well, if the bell wants me to, I'll go."

As sleepy Carl's eyes began to close, he said, "Remember the Sabbath day to keep it holy."

THE GUARDIAN ANGEL.
From a painting by B. Plockhorst.

LESSON XI.

SIN.

"To him therefore that knoweth to do good, and doeth it not, to him it is sin." — Jas. 4 : 17.

WHEN the world had been made ready for people, and God had made man, and given him a wonderful soul that should always live, then he made a beautiful garden for him to live in. In the garden God made "to grow every tree that is pleasant to the sight, and good for food." Gold and beautiful stones were to be found there. The garden was full of sweet flowers. Many different kinds of birds sung wonderful songs. Here, in this lovely garden of Eden, that God had made so pleasant for him, Adam lived.

He "gave names to all cattle, and to the fowl of the air, and to every beast of the field." It must have been very pleasant to Adam to watch the animals, to learn their ways, and to get acquainted with them. As he came to know their lives, and how they cared for themselves, he could give them names that were like them.

Thus Adam lived among the flowers and animals, but he was lonely. The dog and the sheep could not talk to him. He wished to have some one who could understand his thoughts, who could be glad with him, and who could enjoy all the beautiful flowers, the songs of the birds, and the good fruit of the trees.

God knew how lonely Adam was; and he made a woman whom he called Eve, and she lived with Adam, and they were very happy together. They wandered about in the beautiful garden; they watched the flowers as they opened from bud to full bloom. They listened to the different songs of the birds. They saw the squirrels frisking about, and the bees as they flew here and there, gathering honey.

I do not believe the animals were as timid then as they are now. It is because boys and girls, and sometimes men and women, have been unkind and cruel to the animals, that they have become afraid. Do you not believe that Adam and Eve were delighted when they saw the first little kittens?

So the two people spent the happy days watching the many different kinds of animals as they frolicked here and there, or noticing the white clouds as they sailed along against the blue sky. Perhaps one would say to the other, "How kind God is to us to have made the sky with so beautiful colors, and to have the clouds change their shape and color for our pleasure!" Then, perhaps, they would thank God for the fruit which tasted so good to them. Wherever they were, and whatever they were doing, they could always find something good or beautiful that God had made for them. But they did not know of nearly so many wonderful things that God had planned as we know about, and even we have not found all the good things yet.

Sometimes God also walked with them in the garden; and they talked together, and were perfectly happy, because they did only what was right. They were pure and holy, doing just what pleased God.

In the garden was one tree the fruit of which God said they were not to eat. How many of you can think of something that your father or mother says you are not to eat? There were a great many different kinds of fruit-trees, more fruit than Adam and Eve could eat. God knew that it was not best for them to eat the fruit of that tree, and so he told them not to eat it. Surely, when they had the fruit of so many other trees, they would not even think of touching that one.

But they looked at the tree, and thought how good the fruit seemed. Then they kept wishing that they had some. That is where they did wrong. They ought not to have thought any more about the forbidden fruit, but only of the good things that were theirs. When they kept wishing for the fruit, they finally tasted, and then ate. They did what God had told them not to do. They were no longer happy. They hid themselves when God walked in the garden. They were afraid to meet him, because they were no longer holy and pure. They had done wrong, and they knew it; and they knew God must be displeased with them.

MEMORY GEM.

I woke before the morning,
   I was happy all the day,
I never said an ugly word,
   But smiled, and stuck to play.

And now at last the sun is going
   Down behind the wood,
And I am very happy,
   For I know that I've been good.
           — *Robert Louis Stevenson.*

OCCUPATION.

Make the garden of Eden, and place in it tiny branches for trees, one of them to represent the tree of the knowledge of good and evil. Show the children how much better it would have been, had they turned away from the temptation, instead of lingering and looking at the tree.

STORY.—THE FAIRY AND THE GNOME.

"I was just a little thing
    When a fairy came and kissed me;
Floating in upon the light
Of a haunted summer night,
Lo, the fairies came to sing
Pretty slumber songs, and bring
    Certain boons that else had missed me.
From a dream I turned to see
What those strangers brought to me,
    When that fairy up and kissed me;
    Here, upon this cheek, he kissed me."

I wish this little child could have seen the fairy, Fairy Pure Heart, I call her, when she kissed him. Never was there a sweeter face than had Fairy Pure Heart, with her deep, true eyes, her smiling mouth and earnest look. I wish you could know how much she longed to do for the little child when she kissed him. Little Fairy Pure Heart hoped to make his life beautiful; wished to lead him in the right paths, to help him over the rough places. The fairy loved the child so much that she went wherever he did. Hand in hand they wandered, or they lay side by side. When the child slept, the fairy whispered sweet dreams to him,—dreams of helping those about him, and making others happy.

But, if you could have seen sweet Fairy Pure Heart, you would have seen Gnome Unfit, who also was ever hovering around the child. I should be sorry to have you see his face, for it never looked happy. The eyes did not look straight at one, but turned away as if he had done wrong; an ugly frown lay between them, and the mouth did not smile. It was not a pleasant face, so I am glad you could not see it. As the little child grew older, the fairy and the gnome still stayed with him.

He could not see them any more than we can, but he often heard their voices. Fairy Pure Heart's voice was soft and sweet, like the song of a bird, and made the child glad. But the gnome had a very unpleasant voice; and, when he whispered to the child, there came into the face of the child a little look like his, which was not pleasant to see.

The fairy and the gnome were not happy together, for oftentimes Fairy Pure Heart would whisper some pleasant thing to the child, and then Unfit would say just the opposite. Sometimes one would say, "Do this," and the other would say, "No, don't."

One day the child was playing with other children, and wished to play horse, to ride "fierce and fast, till the horse breaks down at last." But the other children wanted to play something else. Fairy Pure Heart whispered, "Do as the others wish;" but Unfit said: "No, don't; you always give in to the others. To play horse is more fun." And the child said to himself, "I won't do what Fairy Pure Heart says; I will do as I want to."

Then the dear fairy was driven a little way off, so that the next time she wished to whisper to the child, she could make him hear only when he was looking toward her. The child felt that Fairy Pure Heart was going away from him; but, instead of telling her he was sorry, and asking her to stay with him, he said, "I do not care if she does go away. I am tired of her."

Then the fairy was driven farther away, until the child no longer heard her voice, and she could only watch him from a long way off. As Fairy Pure Heart was driven away, Unfit was more often listened to by the child, whose face began to look like that of this gnome, who was still with him, disagreeable and cross. The other children did not like to play with the child.

I should not care to tell you this story if the child had always listened to the Gnome Unfit, for the story would be too sad. But sometimes he would not do the wrong thing that Unfit suggested; and then this bad gnome could not whisper so loud, and dear Fairy Pure Heart was glad, and could come nearer the child. She could not get close enough to whisper to him; but she sent beautiful thoughts toward him, and made so sweet music where she was that he caught faint strains of it, and longed to hear more. This made him again think of his Fairy Pure Heart, and he longed to have her come back to him. His very wish for her helped the fairy to come nearer; and, when the child made up his mind that he would not listen to the gnome, but would always try to do what Fairy Pure Heart wished, then she stood close by his side, although he could not see her. Whenever the child was tempted to do what Fairy Pure Heart would not like, she whispered soft and low to him; and the sadness in her voice made him think of the time when she had been so far away from him, and he had been so unhappy; and then he promised her to try harder.

Each one of us has been kissed by the fairy, and each of these two, Fairy Pure Heart and Gnome Unfit, hover about us, to whisper good or bad thoughts. You and I will listen to Fairy Pure Heart, and do all that we can to make her happy, for that is the only way in which we can be happy ourselves.

LESSON XII.

WORK.

"She seeketh wool and flax, and worketh willingly with her hands."
— *Prov. 31 : 13.*

AFTER Adam and Eve had eaten of the fruit of the tree that God had told them not to touch they felt very unhappy. They were no longer glad when they heard God's voice. They did not wish to see him. Can you not feel just how the lump would come in their throats when they tried to speak? And do you not think they wished that they had not touched the fruit? God loved them just the same, and yet they were afraid. They felt as if he did not love them. God was grieved and displeased because they had disobeyed him; yet he loved them.

Whenever we do wrong, we have to suffer the consequences; that is, if we do what is wrong, that naughty thing which we do will someway make us unhappy. Adam and Eve ate of the fruit that God had told them not to touch, and so they could no longer live in the lovely garden, because they might eat of it again. God could not trust them, even though he loved them still. They must go away from the beautiful Eden and never enter it any more.

Before this Adam had kept the garden of Eden; but he had only to care for the different trees bearing fruit, and Adam and Eve had simply to pick the fruit and eat it when they were hungry. But, when they did wrong and could no longer live in this wonderful garden, Adam was obliged to work much harder to get food for them. He dug up the ground, not as the farmers do now, with a plough drawn by a horse; for he did not know how to have the animals help him. It must have been a great deal of work for him to get the land ready to plant the seeds; and then the weeds grew right beside his good plants, and had to be pulled up just as they must be now.

But after a time Adam saw his grain ripen and his vegetables grow large and good to eat, and he was glad, and enjoyed seeing the different plants grow. It is the same with us; if we do our work the very best that we can, we shall be happy in seeing it well done.

God helped Adam just as he helps us now. He sent down the bright, warm rays from the sun to start the tiny seeds buried in the ground; and the gentle drops of rain to help them grow. Whatever we do, God always works with us and helps us.

Suppose sometime the sun should grow tired of shining, and should hide itself for days and days. The beautiful fields of corn and wheat could not grow, neither could the plants and grass. Or, if there should be no rain for weeks, everything would become thirsty and dry. The flowers would droop and hang their heads. The grain would bend over toward the ground instead of standing up tall and straight and growing until it was fit to be made into food for the boys and girls, the men and women, to eat. A great many people would be made unhappy if the sun should stop shining or the rain should not fall again.

Suppose some morning your father should say he was not going to do any work that day. Suppose when the next day came your father should again stay at home, and so on for a week or for two weeks. If he does not go to work, he earns no money; if he has no money, he cannot buy flour from which bread is made, or the milk for you to drink, or the shoes for you to wear. Would you like it if some morning your mother should say: "It is too much work to get up and dress, too much work to care for the children. I think I will not do anything more for them."

This would not do at all, would it? We must each do our own work, whatever it is; however small it may be, it is the work that God has given us to do, and we must each do our part to make his beautiful plan perfect and whole. God has planned for us all to work, and there is a special work ready for each one of us to do. That work is ours, and no one else can do it so well as we, to carry out God's wish. If Frank forgets to bring in the kindlings, and his mother brings them in for him, the fire may burn just as well; but Frank has lost a good gift, because that was his work to do and he did not do it. If he continues to forget, he will not grow up to be as strong and reliable a man as he might have been, and God's plan has not been carried out, just because Frank kept forgetting the wood.

Let us each try to do our own work the very best we can all the time, that we may not be the ones to spoil God's plan.

MEMORY GEM.

A fair little girl sat under a tree,
Sewing as long as her eyes could see;
Then smoothed her work and folded it right,
And said, "Dear work, good night, good night."

OCCUPATION.

Allow the children to plough, harrow, plant, and harvest as our farmers do at present. Bring out the thought that many persons are at work preparing the food we eat.

STORY.—AMY STEWART.

There was once a little girl named Amy Stewart, who liked to play all day in the garden among the flowers and birds. She said they talked to her.

One day her mother said, "You are old enough now, Amy, to do a little work, and you must begin early to be industrious."

"O mamma, I do not like to work; may I not go in the woods and play before I begin to work?"

"As I have nothing ready for you to do just now, you may go for a little while," said her mother.

So Amy ran out-of-doors. A pretty gray squirrel ran across her path, and she called to him, saying, "Dear squirrel, you have nothing to do but play and eat nuts, have you?"

"Yes," said Mr. Squirrel, "I have a large family to support, and I am busy laying up nuts for the winter; so I cannot stop to play with you."

Just then a bee came buzzing by. Amy said, "Little bee, do you have any work to do?"

"It seems to me I have no time for anything but work, getting honey and making the honeycomb."

Amy now saw an ant carrying a crumb of bread.

"Is not that crumb too heavy for you? I wish you would drop it and play with me."

"It is heavy, but I am too glad to get it not to be willing to carry it; but I will stop long enough to tell you about a lazy day we once had. Our house was destroyed, and I was too lazy to help to build it; and I said to my brothers, 'Let us go and travel; perhaps we can find a house ready-made; perhaps the butterflies will play with us.' We travelled a long way, but we found no ready-made house, and at last we were obliged to build one for ourselves. Since then we have been contented to do all the work that we find necessary." The ant then picked up the crumb of bread and hurried away.

Amy sat down on a stone, and thought, "It seems to me all creatures have some work to do, and they seem to like it; but I do not believe flowers have anything to do." So she walked up to a red poppy, and said, "Beautiful red poppy, do flowers work?"

"Of course we do," said the poppy. "I have to take great care to gather all the red rays the good sun sends down to me, and I must keep them in silken petals for you to use; and the green rays must be untangled and held by my glossy leaves; and my roots must drink water, my flowers must watch the days not to let the seed-time pass by, — ah, my child, I assure you we are a busy family, and that is why we are so happy."

Amy walked slowly homeward, and said to her mother: "The squirrels, bees, ants, and even the flowers have something to do. I am the only idle one; please give me some work to do."

Then her mother brought her a towel to hem, which she had begun so long before that she had quite forgotten it. She worked very faithfully, and grew to be an industrious woman, never forgetting that work makes us happier than idleness. — *Anonymous.*

LESSON XIII.

CAIN AND ABEL.

"A wise son maketh a glad father." — *Prov.* 10 : 1.

AFTER a time God gave to Adam and Eve a wonderful gift, one of the most precious things they could possibly have. A baby? Yes, indeed. A dear little son to love and care for, to teach and help. How glad Adam and Eve must have been! What pleasure they must have found in watching the little boy grow! Every little thing that he did, every new cunning way, was as great a joy and pleasure to them as it is to you or your mother while watching your baby.

They called him Cain, which meant a "Possession" to be cared for with all a mother's love, for he was a great gift from God. Adam and Eve loved him greatly. After a little he knew them, and would watch whatever they did, laughing and crowing with glee when they came toward him. By and by he began to walk, to run about among the flowers, and then to talk; and so he grew. Each day his parents loved him more and more, and were delighted with each new thing that he learned to do. To Eve the child was a great comfort and delight, and she watched over him tenderly and cared for him.

Do you suppose he always did what was right? I am afraid not. For even his mother's love could not make him cheerful and kind, loving and unselfish. He wanted to have his own way always. He thought he knew better than any one else, better

MADONNA AND CHILD.
From a painting by Roberto Ferruzzi.

than his own father and mother, better even than God. Do you think he was happy? No, he could not be happy, because he wanted to have his own way and to please himself only.

Adam and Eve had another son after a time, and they called his name Abel, and they loved him even as they had loved Cain. But Abel was not like his brother. As he grew older, no scowl came on his forehead. Abel loved the sunshine and the flowers, the birds that sung, and the lambs that frisked about the meadows. He was happy all day long, and loved to make all about him happy, too. Do you not think Cain must have loved his younger brother Abel, who was so kind and good? Cain did not love him, however, and it was because Abel did what was right, and Cain did not. When we do wrong, we often feel unkind toward those who do right, because in our hearts we know that they are right and we are wrong. But when we begin to do right and are loving and kind, then we love those about us.

Cain and Abel grew to be men. Cain was still sullen and self-willed, while Abel was loving and gentle. Cain ploughed the ground and planted it, and gathered the fruit he had raised. Abel tended the sheep and flocks. I love to think of him as softly playing some instrument, perhaps reeds of different lengths that he had made into pipes, playing soft tunes and singing as he watched the sheep while they fed in the green pastures, or drank water from the flowing brooks.

After a time, the Bible tells us, "Cain brought of the fruit of the ground an offering unto the Lord. And Abel, he also brought of the firstlings of his flock." God had blessed them, and made the fruit to grow and ripen, and the sheep to keep well and strong. It was right for them to give to God a part of what God had helped them to raise. They each built an altar or pile of stones, on which they put their gifts for God. This was called offering sacrifice, and until Jesus came on the earth the people knew no better way; so God was pleased to have them make an offering to thank him for his care.

Cain and Abel each brought the best that he had. But the Bible says, "The Lord had respect unto Abel and to his offering, but unto Cain and to his offering he had not respect." God was pleased with Abel's offering, but not with Cain's. God said to Cain: "Why are you angry? If thou doest well shalt thou not be accepted?" If Cain had loved God, and tried to please him, God would have accepted his offering as well as Abel's. But because Cain felt wicked in his heart God was not pleased with him as he was with Abel, who tried to do right. God could see his heart, and he knew just how Cain felt.

Do you not see that the trouble began when Cain was a little boy and wanted his own way, and scowled and did not try to make others happy? Then, when he grew to be a man, the naughty ways which he had when a boy grew as he grew, until when he became a man God was very much displeased with him. If we want to be good Christian men and women, and to be looked up to and respected by those about us, we must try to be loving, kind, cheerful, and unselfish when we are children. If we do what is right when we are children, we shall do right when we are grown up.

MEMORY GEM.

I pray the prayer of Plato old:
  God make thee beautiful within,
And let thine eyes the good behold
  In everything save sin.
—John G. Whittier.

OCCUPATION.

Let the children build two altars, and place something on them to represent the two offerings. Take pains to have the children clearly understand that Abel's offering was accepted because he himself was good and pleased God, and that Cain's was rejected because his heart was wicked instead of pure and holy.

If more occupation is desired, let one of the children plough and plant the ground, and then take of the harvest for his sacrifice. The two hands can be made into a plough which shall travel up and down an imaginary field. One hand with fingers spread apart will form the harrow. The children can scatter the seed, and so on. Let another child tend the flocks, going with them to the pasture and to the river.

STORY.—THE IMMORTAL FOUNTAIN.

In ancient times two little princesses lived in Scotland, one of whom was very beautiful, the other dark-colored and unpleasant-looking. The two sisters were not happy together. Marion hated Rose because she was handsome, and because every one praised her. Marion scowled and was unkind to all about her. Rose was sweet and loving, always trying to make those about her happy.

Not far from the castle where the two sisters lived was a deep grotto where it was said the queen of the fairies lived. Some persons said Rose had fallen asleep there one day, and that the queen had dipped her into an immortal fountain, from which she had risen with the beauty of an angel. Marion often asked about this, but Rose always answered that she could tell nothing about it.

Marion thought much about the fountain, and at length she went to the grotto. She sat down on a bank of moss and fell asleep. When she awoke it was evening, and she found herself in a small hall with opal pillows about her, and a beautiful rainbow roof. There were brilliant flowers in the beautiful vases. The hall was lighted with thousands of fireflies, flitting about like stars. While Marion was wondering at all this, a figure of rare loveliness stood before her, and sung: —

> "The Fairy Queen
> Hath rarely seen
> Creature of earthly mould
> Within her door,
> On pearly floor,
> Inlaid with shining gold.
> Mortal, all thou seest is fair;
> Quick thy purposes declare."

It seemed as if the birds and the insects joined in the chorus, and between the pauses the sound of a distant waterfall was heard, whose waters fell in music.

Marion answered with a trembling voice, "Will it please your majesty to make me as handsome as my sister Rose?"

"I will do as you ask," answered the queen, "if you will do whatever I say. Go home, and for one week speak no unkind word to your sister. At the end of that time come again to the grotto."

Marion went home very happy. She did not find it easy to be kind and loving to Rose; but, when she felt naughty, she went off by herself, so that she could not speak to Rose, and thus say something unkind. At the end of the week she again went to the grotto, where she found the queen feasting.

When Marion entered, the diamond sparkles on

the wings of the fairies faded as they always did in the presence of anything not perfectly good, and in a few moments the fairies, except the queen, had all flown away, singing : —

> "The Fairy Queen
> Hath rarely seen
> Creatures of earthly mould
> Within her door,
> On pearly floor,
> Inlaid with shining gold."

"Mortal, have you done as I asked?"
"I have," answered Marion.
"Then follow me," continued the queen.

They walked over beds of beautiful flowers. Birds warbled above their heads. Soon they came to a hill where stood a band of fairies clothed in green gossamer, with their ivory wands crossed.

The queen waved her wand over them, and they flew away. The hill was steep; and, as they went up, the air grew more fragrant. At length they were stopped by a band of fairies clothed in blue, with their wands crossed.

"Here," said the queen, "we must stop. You can go no farther now. Go home, and for one month do to your sister just as you would wish her to do to you, were you Rose, and she Marion."

Marion went home again; and, though she found it very hard, she was so anxious to be beautiful that she was sweet and kind to Rose.

Every one noticed how Marion had changed, and Rose said, "I love her dearly."

At the end of the month she went again to the grotto. The fairies in blue lowered their wands and flew away. As Marion and the queen walked on, the path grew steeper and steeper, and the sound of waters falling in music was more clearly heard. They came to a troop of fairies in rainbow robes, with silver wands tipped with gold.

"Go home again," said the queen, "and for three months do not think anything wrong. Then you shall see the immortal fountain."

Marion felt very sad, for she knew that she had often thought wrong things, even if she had not said them. When Marion went to the grotto next, the queen did not smile; and, when they reached the rainbow fairies, the silver specks in their wings grew dim. Marion burst into tears. She knew that wrong thoughts had been in her heart. She went home and tried again. This time the rainbow fairies flew away as she came to them, singing as they went: —

> "Mortal, pass on
> Till the goal is won;
> For such, I ween,
> Is the will of the queen.
> Pass on! Pass on!"

When they came to the beautiful fountain, Marion found purple fairies with golden wands guarding the waters.

Again the queen told her to go home. "For one year," she said, "think no wrong thoughts, not so as to become beautiful, but because it is right."

This was the hardest task of all. Three times she tried and failed, but the fourth time the purple fairies lowered their wands, singing: —

> "Thou hast scaled the mountain,
> Go, bathe in the fountain;
> Rise fair to the sight
> As an angel of light;
> Go, bathe in the fountain."

Marion was about to plunge into the water, when the queen said, "Look in the mirror of the water."

Marion looked, and saw that she was already as beautiful as she could desire.

"The waters of the fountain had been within your soul," said the queen. "The only way to become beautiful is to be unselfish, loving, and kind. A pure heart and right doing are the only immortal fountains of beauty." — *Adapted from L. Maria Child.*

LESSON XIV.

NOAH.

"I do set my bow in the cloud, and it shall be for a token of a covenant between me and the earth." — Gen. 9: 13.

As there came to be more people upon the earth, some of them did wrong and after a while became very wicked. God knew about the wrong things they did, and was grieved. He had made men and women and children with hearts and minds to know what they ought to do, and he wished them to grow like him, pure and holy, always doing right.

When they did wrong, God's Spirit in their hearts tried to lead them to do better; but they would not listen to the little voice within, and still did wrong. Then God sent Noah to show them a better way. Noah and all his family tried to do what would please God. They may have made some mistakes, but they tried to do right. The wicked people grew no better, however, and God could not let them go on doing so much that was wrong, and he determined to destroy them, sending a great flood of water.

God wished Noah and his family to be saved; so he told him to build an ark that could sail upon the water. Perhaps some of the other people helped Noah as he was making the great ark, and very likely they made fun of him, and said that he was foolish to put so much work into it, as there would not be any flood. They had lived a great many years and had never had a flood. But God had told Noah he should send the flood, and Noah believed, and went on building the ark. It took a great while to make so large a vessel, and Noah had plenty of time to urge the people to do right or to save themselves by going with him into the ark. But the wicked people did not believe any harm would come to them, and kept on doing wrong.

God told Noah to take into the ark two of every kind of animal, of beast, of fowl, and of bird, also animals for food for himself and his family; and Noah did as God said. Then he and his wife and his three sons and their wives went into the ark and closed the doors, and after seven days it began to rain. Do you not think the wicked people wished they had listened to Noah and did as he said? As the rain kept on, how sorry they were for their wrongdoing! Instead of being a rain that lasted two or three days, as we sometimes have, it rained all the time for forty days and nights. It rained longer than from Thanksgiving until Christmas. The rivers overflowed and covered the meadows; the water seemed to come from everywhere; the ground began to sink. The waters covered the tops of the trees. By and by they covered the hills. Finally, even the highest mountains were covered with water, and the animals and the people in the ark were the only living beings on the earth, except the fishes and sea-animals. The tents the people lived in, the trees, the flowers, and the grass were all covered by water.

Noah and his family and all the animals in the ark were safe, and after a time it stopped raining. But still they must remain in the ark, because the ground was covered with water. At length, however, God spoke to Noah, saying, "Go forth of the ark, thou, and thy wife, and thy sons, and thy son's wives with thee." God also told him to bring out the animals.

Think of all those animals, — birds, doves, horses, dogs, tigers, lions, sheep, butterflies, all the different kinds coming from the ark down the side of the mountain, for the ark rested on the top of Mount Ararat. They must have been glad to be free once more, and to be able to walk or fly about the earth.

Noah and his family were so grateful that the first thing they did was to thank God for his great care over them. God blessed Noah and his sons, and he said that he would never again let the waters cover the earth, or destroy all the people and animals upon the earth.

God sent the rainbow to show the people that he would remember his promise, and he said: "I do set my bow in the cloud, and it shall be for a token of a covenant between me and the earth. And it shall come to pass, when I bring a cloud over the earth, that the bow shall be seen in the cloud, and I will remember my covenant, which is between me and you and every living creature of all flesh; and the waters shall no more become a flood to destroy all flesh." The covenant is the promise between God and all the people on the earth that he will never send another flood to destroy the world. So whenever you see the rainbow in the sky, you know it is the sign of God's promise to us. By this rainbow we know that he will keep his promise. What a beautiful sign to give us, the lovely bow or arch, with its beautiful colors, — red, orange, yellow, green, blue, and violet! God has always kept his promise. He has made a great many promises in the Bible and never broken one of them.

MEMORY GEM.

Saw the rainbow in the heaven,
In the eastern sky the rainbow,
Whispered, "What is that, Nokomis?"
And the good Nokomis answered,
" 'T is the heaven of flowers you see there;

All the wild-flowers of the forest,
All the lilies of the prairie,
When on earth they fade and perish,
Blossom in that heaven above us."
— *Henry W. Longfellow.*

OCCUPATION.

A Noah's ark and animals, or even paper animals, can be used to illustrate this lesson. If the teacher desires, the raven and the dove can be sent out after the rain has ceased. The animals march down the hill in procession. Too much time and stress should not be laid upon this part of the occupation, however, to the exclusion of the rainbow and promise.

If crayons with square edges of the six standard colors are fastened together in the right order, a beautiful rainbow can be made upon the blackboard with one stroke of the hand.

STORY. — THE RAINBOW PILGRIMAGE.

One summer afternoon I was standing at an eastern window, looking at a beautiful rainbow that, bending from the sky, seemed to be losing itself in a thick, swampy wood about a quarter of a mile away. We had just had a thunder-storm; but now the dark heavens had cleared up, the rose-bushes by the window were dashing rain-drops against the panes, the robins were singing merrily from the cherry-trees, and all was brighter and pleasanter than ever. There was no one in the room with me but my brother Rufus, who had been sick and was sitting in an easy-chair, looking out with me at the rainbow.

"See, brother," said I, "it drops right down among the cedars, where we go in the spring to find wintergreens!"

"Why don't you go to the end of the rainbow, Gracie," said my brother, not supposing that I should think of doing such a thing, "and get the purses filled with the money, and the great pots of gold and silver?"

I at once darted out of the door and started toward the wood. My brother called after me as loudly as he could, but I did not hear him and he could not come after me. I cared nothing for the wet grass that soiled my clean dress and wet my feet as I ran. I felt sure I knew just where that rainbow ended, and I was thinking what fine presents I would give my friends out of my riches.

Almost before I knew it I had reached the cedar grove, and the end of the rainbow was not there. But I saw it shining down among the trees a little farther on; so on and on I struggled, through the thick bushes and over logs, till I came within the sound of the stream which ran through the swamp. I crossed the stream on a fallen tree, and still ran on, although I was tired and it seemed as if I could go no farther. I had forgotten to keep watch of the rainbow; and, when I looked for it again, it was nowhere in sight. It had quite faded away. When I saw that it was indeed gone, I burst into tears; for I had lost all my treasures, and had nothing to show for my pilgrimage but muddy feet and a wet and torn frock. So I set out for home. I was wet, cold, scared, and altogether very miserable. I had lost my way, and wandered about until at last my older brother found me and carried me home. I had been gone nearly three hours and had wandered a number of miles.

When I went into the room where my brother Rufus sat, he said, "Why, my poor little sister! I did not mean to send you off on such a wild-goose chase to the end of the rainbow. I thought you would know I was only quizzing you."

Then my eldest brother took me on his knee, and told me what the rainbow really was; that it was painted air, and did not rest on the earth; so nobody could ever find the end; and that God had set it in the cloud to remind him and us of his promise never again to drown the world with a flood.

"O, I think 'God's promise' would be a beautiful name for the rainbow," I said.

"Yes," replied my mother, "but it tells us something more than that he will not send great floods upon the earth; it tell us of his beautiful love always bending over us from the skies. And I trust that when my little girl sets forth on a pilgrimage to find God's love, she will be led by the rainbow of his promise through all the dark places of this world to treasures laid up in heaven, better, far better, than silver or gold." — *Grace Greenwood.*

MYTH. — IRIS'S BRIDGE.

In the sky, where the amber tints are seen on the clouds, Iris was born. She loved her home and all the beautiful things around her. Perhaps she sailed in the moon's silver boat and knew why the stars kept twinkling. Perhaps she feasted on sunshine and dew, and slept on the soft white clouds.

More than anything in her sky home, Iris loved her grandfather, the stern old ocean. When he was merry, and drove his white horses over the water, she was happy. When he was troubled, and the sky grew dark and sad, she quietly slipped her hand into his. Instantly he smiled, and became gentle again. He longed always to keep her with him, but the sun said: "No, Iris belongs to both ocean and sky. Let her be the messenger between heaven and earth."

They placed golden wings upon her shoulders, and made her a bridge of beautiful colors. One end of the bridge they rested in the sky, but the other Iris fastened to the earth. This was the way Iris's path was made: the earth gave the tints of the fairest flowers, the sea brought great ribbons of silvery mist, the wind was the shuttle, the sky was the loom, and the sun himself was the weaver.

It is no wonder that the most beautiful thing in the world is Iris's bridge, the rainbow.

LESSON XV.

EASTER.

"*I shall be satisfied, when I awake, with thy likeness.*" — Ps. 17 : 15.

We have talked about the world when it was new, about the trees as they grew, and about the flowers and different plants. Do you not think it must have been something like another new world when Noah came out of the ark? The water had destroyed everything. Trees, plants, and grass were all gone. Then it began to grow green again. How beautiful it must have looked to Noah after being shut up in the ark so many, many days! If we had never seen anything green, how delighted we should be with even a little patch of grass! How we should watch it each day, and how pleased we should be over every new spear of grass that started! If we could get so much pleasure from just a little grass, what would it be like to see the trees grow green, the vines put out leaves, and all the earth put on a beautiful green dress?

Let us think of the earth as it would look if there were no plants and grass growing. Suppose the world all looked like the streets in front of your houses, — dirt, dirt everywhere, and no grass. Would the earth be as pretty if the trees had no leaves? Think of the oak-tree, with its gnarled branches all bare and the wind blowing through them; think of leafless birch and elm trees, with their long, slender branches swaying in the wind and showing bare against the sky. They are pretty even that way, the branches are so graceful; but how glad we are to see the leaves on them! Suppose we take away all the flowers, goldenrod and asters, daisies and buttercups, the pretty vines and bushes; would the earth be as beautiful to you? Should you like to live in such a place all the time? Should you like to see the world bare the year round?

Suppose you lived where all was brown and bare; and then some day you should find little buds on the trees, and these should grow and grow each day, and after a little time tiny green shoots should begin to spring up out of the ground here and there, what would you think? I know you would be delighted, and would watch the plants and trees each day. The buds would grow larger and larger until they burst out, some into leaves, some into flowers, until, after a little, all the earth would become beautiful.

If we had never seen this happen, should we not think it very wonderful for the brown, dead-looking earth suddenly to grow green and beautiful and covered with lovely flowers, and the trees to put forth green leaves on every branch and twig? Yet this happens every year. Through winter the trees are bare, the grass and plants look dead; they are brown and lifeless. All winter they remain so; but, when the warm weather comes, then the buds open, and the leaves burst forth. One by one the flowers open to the sun; little by little the whole earth is clothed in green, and looks like a different place. All this wonderful change has been made for us. Is it any less wonderful because God brings to new life the trees and plants year after year, than if he did it only once? Does it not show greater power to be able to do this every year? How beautiful a lesson for us that God does not tire of making the earth blossom and grow beautiful each spring!

Let us watch the trees and plants this spring as they bud and blossom for us. Let us notice the beautiful shapes and colors, the difference between the various kinds of buds and leaves; let us never forget that the same God who made the earth in the beginning makes it grow green and beautiful each spring.

I want to tell you one more wonderful thing about God. He can make just as great a change in us as he does on the earth when the trees grow green and the plants blossom and all becomes beautiful. Our hearts are like the bare earth in winter-time, but by and by God will take us to live with him, and our hearts will become beautiful as does the earth in the springtime. God says that we cannot know what we shall be like then, for he will make us like himself. We have never seen God, but we know that he is perfectly good and loving, that he is holy and pure; and he has promised that we shall be like him.

The little seeds of love are in our hearts now, and if we water them, that is, if we try to please God, by and by they will blossom into beautiful flowers, just as the plants do in the spring on the earth. God will make them more beautiful than any flowers we ever saw. This is why we are so glad at Easter, because God will some day make us like himself, pure and holy, and beautiful as the Easter lilies we all love so much.

MEMORY GEM.

Lo! the winter is past;
The flowers appear again on the earth;
The time of the singing of the birds is come,
And their voices are heard in all our land.
The trees put forth their leaves,
And the buds break into blossom.
Consider the lilies how they grow,
And the roses how they bloom.

OCCUPATION.

There is a little toy called Japanese water-lilies that will make an excellent illustration for this lesson. The flowers come in a little wooden box, and look like tiny wooden sticks an inch or an inch and a half long. When placed in water, they expand and look like leaves and flowers. They are colored and very pretty, and interest the children greatly. Eight or ten different kinds are to be found in a box, and the price is but five cents.

After children have begun to see the wonder and beauty of the new life God gives to nature, they will be better able, when older, to grasp and accept the stupendous truth of the resurrection.

STORY.—THE WONDERFUL CHANGE.

It is a beautiful warm day in June. Most of the birds that love the pond and the bushes that grow near it have selected their homes, and have either built their nests or are just beginning them. If one watches closely, the bright flash of color can be seen as the red-winged blackbird darts down to its nest. He has given his early morning call of "Kronk-a-ree," and has now settled to work to find food for his mate who is busy at the nest. The white swamp honeysuckle has begun to open its buds, making all the air fragrant with its sweet odor. Along the edges of the pond are to be seen the green spires of the blue flag with its large blue-purple flowers, variegated with yellow or white. Above these hovers the bee, which soon alights upon the curved sepal, and thrusts its head inside the flower to find the hidden nectar. See how dusty he is as he flies away to another flower. This is what the blossom wished. It wanted him to carry its pollen to another blossom.

Darting about upon the water are the water-spiders, while above its surface the bright blue dragon-fly flutters and sails along as gracefully as any bird. Down in the mud at the bottom of the pond crawls a clumsy black bug. He knows nothing of all the beautiful things above him. He can simply crawl about, catching and eating the little flies and mosquitoes that are so unfortunate as to get within his reach. He is not very attractive, but he is doing the best he can and knows nothing of a better life.

After a time the black bug has a strange feeling come over him. He no longer cares for the flies and mosquitoes. He does not feel hungry. He cannot tell what is the matter with him, but he feels that he must get away from the mud and slime of the bottom of the pond, and he crawls up one of the slippery stems of the blue flag near him. It is not easy for him to do this, but at last he reaches the top and creeps out of the water, still clinging to the stout stem of the blue flag. Why does he not skip about as do the other bugs or the spiders upon the surface of the water? Poor thing, he cannot. He is not used to being out of the water, and the warm sun makes his skin dry and hard and too tight for him. He feels so weak and tired that he knows not what to do; still, he clings to the green stalk of the blue flag. Soon he begins to twist and turn; and, as he does so, a part of his skin is loosened and slips over his eyes so that he can see nothing. Finally it is pushed entirely off, and he finds that he has a new face under the old one and that he can see with new eyes; in fact, they are much finer than were the old ones.

As he looks about, the beautiful blossoms of the blue flag by his side seem a deeper, richer shade of blue, and the leaves more graceful; he discovers the white blossoms of the honeysuckle and for the first time notices its fragrance. He lifts his head to see more of this wonderful new world, and, as he does so, he draws himself out of his old skin and discovers that he has two pairs of wings of thinnest gauze and beautiful color. At first they are weak, but after a little he finds that they are wondrously strong in spite of their delicate appearance.

At last the clumsy black bug has crawled entirely out of its old skin, and finds himself a slender blue dragon-fly like the ones we have seen skimming over the pond so gayly. When he has rested a while, he, too, lifts his wings and darts here and there, skimming about for the mere pleasure of the motion. He flies to the sweet blossoms of the swamp honeysuckle, and thinks how wonderful it is that all these beauties were here before and he knew nothing about them. He dips down to the blue flag, and looks at the stem up which he had crawled with so much difficulty a short time before. He sees the red-winged blackbird as she darts to her nest, and soon learns to know the songs of the various birds. Life seems a wonderful, a glorious, thing to the bright dragon-fly, and he is thankful every moment for the change that has come to him. There are other black bugs down at the bottom of the pond, which know nothing about the life he leads; but some day they will be changed as he was, and begin a new and beautiful life.

LESSON XVI.

ABRAHAM.

"The father of a multitude of nations have I made thee." — Gen. 17 : 5.

To-day we are to talk about another one of God's people whom he had promised to bless greatly. His name was Abraham. He and his wife Sarah lived in tents in the country of Canaan, and had many servants and cattle and sheep. The servants cared for the cattle ; they fed and watered them ; when it was the right time of year, they sheared the sheep; the women made cloth of the wool, which was afterward made into garments for the men and women.

Do you suppose that God promised to bless Abraham because he was rich? No, it was because Abraham loved God and tried to do what would please God. The people about him did not love God, and God could not be pleased with them when they did not do what was right.

God promised Abraham that he would give him and his children and their children all the land about him. He promised that all the land he could see to the west of him, to the east of him, to the north and to the south of him, should sometime belong to his children. God also promised to bless him and his children and their children greatly.

Now Abraham and Sarah had no children, and they wished very much for a little son. They would have been glad to give some of their servants and some of their cattle and sheep, if only they could have a child of their own.

One day, when Abraham was sitting in the tent door, while it was very warm in the sun, he looked up and saw three men, "and when he saw them, he ran to meet them from the tent door, and bowed himself to the earth, and said, My lord, if now I have found favor in thy sight, pass not away, I pray thee, from thy servant: let now a little water be fetched, and wash your feet, and rest yourselves under the tree: and I will fetch a morsel of bread, and comfort ye your heart; after that ye shall pass on: forasmuch as ye are come to your servant."

This was the way in which people received strangers and welcomed them to their homes in the East. It seems a very friendly and pretty way. Abraham wished to do everything that he could for them. After they had eaten of the food he brought them, which was the best he had, the three men told Abraham that he and Sarah should surely have a little son.

How wonderful a promise this was! Abraham and Sarah were old people; they had lived a long time, and, though they had wanted to have a little child, they thought they had grown too old. Now God promised to give them a son. God always keeps his promise, and he kept this one. Abraham and Sarah did have a son, and they called his name Isaac. They loved him very much. God had told Abraham that his children's children should become a great nation, that there should be a great many of them, and that he would do wonderful things for them; they should be his people.

Abraham tried to teach Isaac to do what was right, to please God. He knew that, if Isaac did wrong, probably Isaac's children would also do wrong. If Isaac pleased God in all his ways, his children would be more likely to please God.

Did you ever think that when you do wrong, not

only do you displease God, but very likely you lead some one else to do wrong also? Some little boy or girl sees you do the wrong thing, and he does the same naughty thing. Not only have you done something wrong, but you have made some one else naughty also.

It is just as true that when you try to do right you help others to be better. If one child in school pays attention and does not whisper, the next boy will be less likely to whisper, and that will help another child, so that in time all the children in the room are better.

You and I are going to try to see how many times we can do right, and so lead some one else to do what is right. We are going to be careful not to set any one else a bad example.

MEMORY GEM.

I shot an arrow into the air,
It fell to earth, I knew not where;
For, so swiftly it flew, the sight
Could not follow it in its flight.

I breathed a song into the air,
It fell to earth, I knew not where;
For who has sight so keen and strong
That it can follow the flight of song?

Long, long afterward, in an oak
I found the arrow, still unbroke;
And the song, from beginning to end,
I found again in the heart of a friend.
— *Henry W. Longfellow.*

OCCUPATION.

Make cardboard tents for Abraham and his servants to live in. Have something to represent

Abraham sitting in the tent doorway when the three men come in sight. Abraham should be made to go and meet them, and servants should then bring water to wash the feet (explain this custom), and also food for their refreshment.

STORY.—RUPERT'S DREAM.

"Look carefully," said nurse, turning down the corner of the flannel blanket. "Don't touch her, dears, but just look."

Mary and Rupert stood on tiptoe and peeped into the tiny red face. They were frightened at first, the baby was so very small.

"Look at her little hands," whispered Mary. "Aren't they lovely? O, I do wish I could give her a hug!"

"Not yet," said nurse. "She is too tender to be hugged. But mamma says you can give her something. She wants to tell you about it. You may both go very quietly to mamma, while she talks with you."

Mary and Rupert stole quietly to the side of their mother, who said: "I cannot talk much, dears, but I want to ask you to help me about baby. Mamma is very anxious that each of her three dear children shall grow up to be a noble, loving, unselfish man or woman. Mamma wants to ask Mary and Rupert to help her teach the dear little baby sister to become sweet and kind and gentle. You can do quite as much to make her good as mamma can. Would you like to try?"

"Yes, mamma; but how can we?" asked Rupert.

"By always doing what is right yourselves. If baby sees you trying to help mamma, she will try; if she sees you unselfishly giving up to others and making others happy, she will grow unselfish; but, if she sees you cross and unkind, she will quickly grow unkind too."

"I will teach her what is right, mamma. I will be good," said Rupert.

Then nurse came and led the children back to their play, that they might not make mamma tired. Mary and Rupert talked it over, and decided that they would try very hard.

The baby grew very slowly, it seemed to the children. They did not see how they could ever teach her to be good, for she did not notice anything they did. She was only a baby. After a time they almost forgot about the little talk mamma had with them. Two years seems a long time to children.

One day when Baby Nell was two years old, Rupert ran into the house from his play; and, when mamma asked him to please hang up his things, he made up a cross face. He wanted to play with his sister Mary's doll, and his mother said, "No, I am afraid you will break it." Then Rupert stamped his little foot, and said, "I won't." Mamma was obliged to put him in the closet; but when she came back Baby Nell had Mary's doll, and when mamma asked her to lay it upon the table, Baby Nell stamped her tiny foot, and said, "I won't," just as near as she could like what Rupert had said.

That night, when mamma was putting Rupert to bed, she told him how baby had been naughty, and said just the same thing that he had said. She reminded him of the time when Nell was a tiny little baby, and he had promised to help her teach baby to do right.

"Would you like to have your little sister grow up to be cross, to scold and fret and pout, to stamp her foot and say naughty things? Think how bad it makes mamma feel."

Rupert was really sorry, and before he fell asleep

he made up his mind that he would try never to do anything that mamma would not like to see Baby Nell doing.

All at once Rupert thought he was his mother, and that Baby Nell was as old as he had been before he became mamma. He looked at Baby Nell, and her little face was as dirty as could be. Of course he would not like to have his little girl with so dirty a face, for he was mamma; and so he tried to wash it clean. Baby Nell stamped her foot, and screamed and cried, and he did not know what to do.

Then he thought she got Mary's new book, and began to mark on it with a pencil, and, when he tried to take it away from her, she threw it on the floor and broke the cover off. Next, she seemed to be sitting at the table and holding her bread with both hands, and picking up her meat with her fingers instead of her fork. He tried to tell her pleasantly that she ought not to eat in that way, but she only looked cross, and then made up a face. "O, O, dear! what shall I do?"

"What is the matter, my little boy?" asked his mother.

"O mamma, I had such a horrid dream!" but almost before he had said the words he was asleep again and dreaming. This time he was himself, little Rupert, and he was sitting at the table and eating his bread so nicely that his mamma smiled at him. He thought he looked at Baby Nell, and she, too, was holding her bread in one hand, and eating like a little lady. Then it seemed as if Nell wanted his sister Mary's paint-box, and he was afraid that she was going to be naughty about it; so he ran and got his box of colored pencils and a paper, and said, "See, Nell, what Rupert is going to do." He began to draw a picture of a little girl with a face so sunny and bright-looking that Baby Nell laughed right out, and Rupert was surprised to find that the face he had drawn in his dream looked just like his baby sister's.

He woke up thinking about it. As he thought of the first dream, he felt like crying. It had been so bad. He had not known what to do, and was having so hard a time. But, when he thought of the second dream, he wondered whether his mamma felt as happy when the children did right as he did in his second dream. Then he wondered whether she felt as much like crying when they were naughty as he did in his first dream. Rupert made up his mind that the second dream should come true. He decided that he would help his mother teach Baby Nell what was right, that he would always do right himself. It was hard work, but mamma's happy face gave him so much pleasure that he kept on trying, until finally one night she said to him, "I am sure Rupert is really trying to set Nell a good example."

O, how happy a little boy was Rupert that night!

LESSON XVII.

ISAAC.

"Her children rise up, and call her blessed." — Prov. 31 : 28.

Do you remember that after God made Adam he said, "It is not good that the man should be alone; I will make him an helpmeet for him"? God made a woman to be Adam's wife, to help him and bless him in order that together they might make a happy home. Ever since then God has been pleased when new homes have been begun, and has greatly blessed husbands and wives who love each other and try to do what is right.

Abraham had left his friends and gone to a new country as God had told him. His son Isaac grew to be a man, and Abraham did not wish him to marry any of the women who lived near, for they did not know and love God. If we are to be God's children and to do what will please him, it is best for us to be with people who are also trying to do what he wishes. So Abraham desired his son Isaac to have some one who knew and loved God for his dearest friend, for his wife. He, therefore, called one of his servants, whom he greatly trusted, and told him to go to the country where they used to live to find a wife for Isaac, one who should really be a blessing and help to him. Then the servant took ten of Abraham's camels, and went toward the country where Abraham had once lived. He wished to do the best he could to find the woman who would

REBECCA AT THE WELL.
From a painting by Frederick Goodall.

make the very best wife for Isaac; so he asked God to help him. In those days God often helped his people in a different way from what he does now. He sometimes told them by dreams what he wished them to do, sometimes in other ways. People then did not have the Bible to tell them what is right.

When Abraham's servant reached the country, he prayed to God and asked him to show him which woman he wished to be Isaac's wife. It was evening and the women went to the well at that time of day to draw water, for they had no water in their houses. The servant prayed God to send the right woman and to show him when she came. He prayed that she might reply to him, when he asked her for a drink of water, "Drink, and I will give thy camels drink also." In this way he would know that he had found the right one. God did as he asked. Before the servant had finished praying a woman called Rebekah came with her pitcher upon her shoulder.

The servant ran to meet her, and said, "Give me to drink, I pray thee, a little water of thy pitcher," and she said, "Drink, my lord." Then she gave his camels water also. Thus the servant knew that God had heard and answered his prayer.

He gave Rebekah costly presents, and went home with her, and was kindly received by her brother Laban. He told of his master Abraham and his son Isaac, and how Abraham wished his son to have a wife from among the people where he used to live. Then Laban said that it should be as God wished, and told the servant that Rebekah might go with him. Then the servant gave her more beautiful jewels, and he also gave precious things to her mother and to Laban. They asked Rebekah whether she would go with the servant and be Isaac's wife, and she said, "I will go." So she went with the servant back to Abraham's home. As they came near, Isaac saw them coming, and hastened to meet them. Then Rebekah looked up and saw Isaac, and she got down from the camel and asked the servant who the man was. He told her that it was his master.

The Bible does not tell us much more about Isaac and Rebekah at that time, except that Isaac took her to his mother's tent, and that she became his wife and he loved her. But do you know how much those few words mean? Isaac and Rebekah were to live together all the rest of their lives; and, if they had not loved each other, they would have been very unhappy. When we really love some one, we wish to do just what will please that person. So Rebekah and Isaac tried to make each other happy. God means that the family shall all love one another, that father shall love mother and mother love father, that children shall love their parents and the parents love the children. This makes a happy family, and helps to carry out God's great plan.

MEMORY GEM.

This is the mother so busy at home,
Who loves her dear children, whatever may come.

This is the father, so brave and strong,
Who works for his family all the day long.

This is the brother, who'll soon be a man;
He helps his good mother as much as he can.

This is the sister, so gentle and mild,
Who plays that the dolly is her little child.

This is the baby, all dimpled and sweet,
How soft his wee hands and his chubby, pink feet!

Father, and mother, and children so dear,
Together you see them, one family here.

OCCUPATION.

Build the well with blocks, and bring Abraham's servant on his camel from one direction, while Rebekah comes from the other with her water-pitcher on her shoulder. Then the servant may accompany her to her brother's tent, and finally they may both go back to Abraham's home where they are met by Isaac.

STORY.—THE CHILDREN'S HOUR.

Between the dark and the daylight,
   When the night is beginning to lower,
Comes a pause in the day's occupations,
   That is known as the Children's Hour.

I hear in the chamber above me
   The patter of little feet,
The sound of a door that is opened,
   And voices soft and sweet.

From my study I see in the lamplight,
   Descending the broad hall stair,
Grave Alice, and laughing Allegra,
   And Edith with golden hair.

A whisper, and then a silence:
   Yet I know by their merry eyes
They are plotting and planning together
   To take me by surprise.

A sudden rush from the stairway,
   A sudden raid from the hall!

By three doors left unguarded
   They enter my castle wall!

They climb up into my turret
   O'er the arms and back of my chair;
If I try to escape, they surround me;
   They seem to be everywhere.

They almost devour me with kisses,
   Their arms about me entwine,
Till I think of the Bishop of Bingen
   In his Mouse-Tower on the Rhine!

Do you think, O blue-eyed banditti,
   Because you have scaled the wall,
Such an old mustache as I am
   Is not a match for you all?

I have you fast in my fortress,
   And will not let you depart,
But put you down into the dungeon
   In the round-tower of my heart.

And there will I keep you forever,
   Yes, forever and a day,
Till the walls shall crumble to ruin,
   And moulder in dust away!

—*Henry W. Longfellow.*

LESSON XVIII.

JACOB.

"Of all that thou shalt give me I will surely give the tenth unto thee." — Gen. 28:22.

In our last lesson we learned how Abraham sent his servant to find a wife for his son Isaac from among the people who knew and served God. The people among whom Isaac lived still worshipped idols, and when Jacob, the son of Isaac and Rebekah, became a man, he went to his mother's old home, that he might find a wife among God's people.

There was no train for him to take, for people did not know how to make or run an engine. He did not go in a carriage, even; he walked. There was no hotel for Jacob to stay at over night, and when the sun had set, and it began to grow dark, he took a stone and put it under his head for a pillow, and lay down to sleep.

The people in that country used to believe that when they dreamed the dream meant something, and that whatever they saw in the dream would come true. They did not have the Bible to teach them about God and what was right, as we have, and it may be that God sometimes sent dreams in order to teach some truth.

While Jacob lay asleep on the hard ground, with nothing but a stone upon which to rest his head, he dreamed, "and behold a ladder set up on the earth, and the top of it reached to heaven: and behold the angels of God ascending and descending on it. And, behold, the Lord stood above it, and said, I am the

Lord, the God of Abraham thy father and the God of Isaac: the land whereon thou liest, to thee will I give it, and to thy seed; and thy seed shall be as the dust of the earth, and thou shalt spread abroad to the west, and to the east, and to the north, and to the south: and in thee and in thy seed shall all the families of the earth be blessed. And, behold, I am with thee, and will keep thee whithersoever thou goest, and will bring thee again into this land; for I will not leave thee, until I have done that which I have spoken to thee of."

Could God have sent him a more beautiful dream than the broad shaft of a light streaming down from heaven to earth, looking like a ladder, and the wonderful white-robed angels going up and down, as if to show him that heaven was not far from earth? Above it stood the Lord, and talked with Jacob. He told him that he would go with him, and keep him from all danger; he promised to bring him safely back, and to give him and his children and their children all the land round about him; and, more than all this, God promised to bless him.

When Jacob awoke, he said, "Surely the Lord is in this place, and I knew it not." Then Jacob knew that it was a holy place, and he said, "This is none other but the house of God, and this is the gate of heaven." There was no church there, but Jacob called it the house of God and the gate of heaven. Wherever God is, that place becomes his house. When boys and girls, or men and women, love God so much that he comes and lives with them, then their hearts become his house.

"Jacob rose up early in the morning, and took the stone that he had put under his head, and set it up for a pillar, and poured oil upon the top of it." And Jacob said, "If God will be with me, and will keep me in this way that I go, and will give me bread to eat, and raiment to put on, so that I come again to my father's house in peace, then shall the Lord be my God, and this stone, which I have set up for a pillar, shall be God's house: and of all that thou shalt give me I will surely give the tenth unto thee."

Jacob had left his home, and was going to a distant country; he was going all alone where he had never been before. He did not know what might happen to him, or whether he would ever reach his home, and see his dear father and mother again. But when God sent him this beautiful vision, and promised to go with him all the way and to bless him so greatly, he felt that he could not do enough to show God how thankful he was. He would always try to do what God wished, and he would try to use whatever God gave him, money or sheep and cattle, to please God, and to help those who had less than he.

If Jacob felt that he owed God so much, how much do you think boys and girls now ought to do for the heavenly Father who has given them such beautiful homes, loving fathers and mothers to care for them, so many, many good things that Jacob did not even know about, and, more than all, the Bible and the dear Christ to help them to do what is right?

MEMORY GEM.

Now is the time to begin to do right;
To-day, whether skies be dark or bright,
Make others happy by deeds of love,
Looking up always for help from above.

OCCUPATION.

Let the occupation for this lesson be very simple, and strive to make the word-picture of the ladder, with its heavenly forms and the God of all standing above, as vivid and impressive as possible. Make Isaac's tent at one side of the table, and let Jacob bid his father and mother and brother good-by and start alone. Let one of the children arrange the stone upon which he rests his head to sleep, and leave the illustration here, to carry on the story of the vision.

STORY.—IN HEAVEN.

Beyond the stars, across the blue,
The angel babies, peeping through,
Look down from heaven and smile on you,
And wish that you were up there, too.

They like to live away up high;
They like to float across the sky;
They're always glad, and that is why
They think it isn't sad to die.

But free as birds upon the wing,
And fair as flowers that ope in spring,
They carol round their Saviour King;
His glory lights them while they sing.

You'd almost be afraid to go?
You've never been up there, I know;
I'd rather have you wait, and grow
To be a man on earth below.

— *From "Twilight Stories," by Elizabeth E. Foulke.*
By permission of Silver, Burdett, & Company, publishers.

STORY.—STAR DOLLARS.

Once upon a time there was a little girl whose father and mother were dead, and she became so poor that she had no roof to shelter herself under, and no bed to sleep in; and at last she had nothing left but the clothes on her back, and a loaf of bread in her hand, which a compassionate person had given to her.

But she was a good and pious little girl; and, when she found herself forsaken by all the world, she went out into the fields, trusting God.

Soon she met a poor man, who said to her, "Give me something to eat, for I am so hungry!" She handed him the whole loaf, and with a "God bless you!" walked on further.

Next she met a little girl crying bitterly, who said to her, "Pray give me something to cover my head with, for it is so cold." She took off her bonnet and gave it away.

In a little while she met another child who had no cloak, and to her she gave her own frock.

By that time it was growing dark, and our little girl entered a forest; presently she met a fourth maiden, who begged something, and to her she gave her petticoat. "For," thought our heroine, "it is growing dark, and nobody will see me; I can give away this."

Now she had scarcely anything left to cover herself. But just then some of the stars fell down in silver dollars, and among them she found a petticoat of the finest linen. In that she collected the starmoney, which made her rich all the rest of her life.
— *Grimm's "Household Tales."*

LESSON XIX.

JOSEPH THE BOY.

"Behold, how good and how pleasant it is for brethren to dwell together in unity." — Ps. 133: 1.

ALL through the Bible we read much of Abraham, Isaac, and Jacob, because they were the first ones to be called God's people. Jacob had twelve sons, one of whom I want to tell you about. His name was Joseph, and he was the next to the youngest. He and Benjamin, the youngest, were greatly loved by their father because they were the youngest, because when he became an old man they were little boys, while the other sons were grown up. I think there is also another reason why Joseph's father loved him more than his older sons. Joseph was a better son; he was more loving and unselfish and kind. Jacob gave Joseph a beautiful coat, different from any that his brothers had; and they did not think that this was right.

One night not long after this, Joseph dreamed a most strange dream. He thought that he was in the field with his brothers, and that they were gathering the grain into sheaves; that is, they were tying the grain into bundles, that they might carry it home more easily. Joseph dreamed that his sheaf of grain stood upright, and that the other sheaves, the ones that his brothers had bound, all bowed down to his sheaf, as if they wished to honor him. Joseph told his dream to his brothers, and they were angry with him; for they thought it meant that they were to be his servants. Not long after this, Joseph dreamed again; and this time he thought that the sun, the moon, and eleven stars bowed down to him. When he told this dream, his brothers were even more angry, and his father reproved him, and said, "Shall I and thy mother and thy brethren indeed come to bow down ourselves to thee to the earth?"

Do you remember that I told you that Cain kept the wicked thoughts in his heart and so grew worse and worse? This is just what Joseph's brothers did. They kept on being angry with Joseph until the wicked thoughts in their hearts had grown so big that they were ready to do any cruel thing to him, their own brother.

Jacob had a great many flocks, and, when the sheep had eaten all the grass near home, the older sons went off a long way to find new pasture for them. Jacob wished to hear from his sons, to know whether they were well; so he sent Joseph to find them. Joseph wandered about some time, but did not find his brothers. At last a man told him where they were, and Joseph followed after them. When his brothers saw him coming, instead of being glad to see him and thankful for the food he had brought them and pleased because their father had sent their brother to learn whether they were well, they said to one another, "Here comes the dreamer." They felt very angry in their hearts because of his dreams, because they thought they were just as good as he, and they let the bad thoughts grow worse.

Some of the brothers were so angry with him that they wanted to hurt him, but Reuben, the oldest brother, said, "No, let us not do him any harm; but we will put him into this pit," a great empty hole there was near by, "and leave him there." Perhaps Reuben was not so cruel as his brothers, for in his heart he thought that after the other brothers had gone on he would take Joseph up out of the pit and take him home to his father.

Then Reuben went off to another part of the field; and, while he was gone, a band of merchants who were carrying goods to sell in Egypt came by, and Judah, one of the brothers, said to the others, "Let us sell Joseph to these people instead of leaving him in the pit." They drew their brother up out of the hole, and gave him to the men for money. If they had not allowed the wicked thoughts toward Joseph to be in their hearts, they could not have done so cruel a thing as to sell their own brother. But, when we let ourselves be angry with some one else, and let ourselves think naughty and wicked thoughts, then we cannot tell what awful things we may do.

When Reuben came back and looked for Joseph in the pit, and did not find him, he felt very sad. He had not wished to hurt his brother, and had intended to take him back to his father after a little time.

When the brothers returned home without Joseph, Jacob grieved for him a long time, he had loved Joseph so much. Another time we shall see what became of Joseph.

MEMORY GEM.

A little bit of patience often makes the sunshine come
And a little bit of love makes a very happy home.

OCCUPATION.

Let the brothers be tending the sheep at some distance from Jacob's tents. Joseph should be made to search for them, and, when he at length finds them, be cast into the pit. After this the Midianites' caravan comes up, and Joseph is sold and carried off.

STORY. — THE LILY-PIPE.

"The bubbles won't stay!" cried Johnny. There were tears in his eyes. He had come out on the lawn to make soap-bubbles. Kate and Willie had been making them before they started for school. Johnny had been trying to do just as Willie did, but the bubbles always burst when he tried to toss them off.

He stood looking across the flower-bed toward the street. He wished Willie were near enough to help him.

"Why, what is that?" he cried in surprise. "Is the sun coming down from the sky?" He winked the tears away and looked again. "Why, it's a golden bubble, and it's coming this way. It has passed the pine-tree already!"

It sunk lower and lower; and, when it came near, it broke, and silvery clouds came rolling out of it. In the midst of the clouds there was a pretty little girl. Her golden ringlets were as fine and soft as silk. They blew about her face as she came moving toward him.

She held a pretty pipe in her hand. "Try this," she said, smiling and looking at Johnny. "The bubbles blown from it will never break. It will make pretty pictures."

Johnny took it gladly. It looked like a golden lily with a hollow stem. It was beautiful. How kind the little girl had been to bring it! Johnny would ask her to stay and play with him. He looked up. His face was all aglow with thanks.

But there was no little girl there, nor any silvery

clouds, nor golden bubble! Was it a dream? Johnny half believed it was. "But no, I have the pipe," he said; "I shall try it, anyhow!"

The first bubble Johnny blew with his pipe showed the picture of the little girl who gave it. It did not float away. It was held fast by a golden thread. The thread came from the pistil of the lily. As Johnny blew, the thread grew longer.

"This bubble makes a very pretty kite," thought Johnny. He broke the thread and tied it to a lilac-bush. Then he blew another bubble. Soon he had a dozen of them flying from the bush. When Johnny had grown tired of his pipe, he put it away in the garret for a while. But, whenever he had a pretty thought, he would bring it down again and blow a bubble. Johnny hid his bubbles in the garret. He was shy about having people see them, but he always showed them to his mother. They would go together and tie them to the rafters. On one of the bubbles was a garden of roses, with fairies, like butterflies, flitting among the flowers. There were pictures of the stories that Johnny loved to hear. The faces of the friends he knew looked fairer in the bubbles.

One bubble seemed to Johnny the prettiest of all. It showed his mother's picture as she looked when he had pleased her.

One day late in the summer Johnny came running into the house. "O, mamma," he cried, "may I go in swimming?"

But his mother shook her head. "No, Johnny," she said; "the water is too cold."

Now, Johnny had wished to go very much, and, besides, he hated to tell the boys, who waited at the gate, that his mother had said he should not go. The boys had told him, when he started to the house, that they never had to ask to go in swimming. It took

Johnny a long time to walk back to the gate. He looked down all the way to hide his tears.

"Mamma says I must n't go," he said, in a low voice. He did not dare to look up. He felt ashamed to have the boys know how he was feeling.

"Why don't you go anyhow?" asked little Sammie Horner. He felt sorry for Johnny, and he wanted him to go. "You can slip off through the garden, and she will never know!"

"No," said Johnny, "I would n't run off!" He meant to do right, even if it was hard.

The big boy looked vexed. "Well, stay, and be a baby!" he said, as he started down the street. He hated little Johnny for being a better boy than he was. So he laughed at him with the other boys. Johnny could hear them laughing as he ran into the house. He was angry now. How his cheeks burned! His mother sat sewing by the window.

"Mamma," he cried, "you are real mean not to let me go!"

His mother looked up, but she did not speak. Johnny wished that she would say something. He started off up-stairs, slamming the door as he went. He never stopped until he reached the garret.

There hung his pipe among the cobwebs. He had not seen it for a long time. He took it down and began to blow a bubble. He had never before tried to make one when he felt cross. He blew hard, and now a strange thing happened. This bubble, instead of rising as the others had done, hung downward from the lily bell.

He took the pipe from his mouth to look. What do you guess he saw upon the bubble? It was a fierce tiger with open mouth showing white, cruel teeth! It looked eager to bite. "O!" cried Johnny, covering his eyes with his hands, "I did n't know my thoughts would look like that!" He wished that he could hide the bubble. What if mamma should see it! He took it to the window and broke the thread.

The bubble fell at his feet with a thud. "It will never fly away," cried Johnny; "what shall I do?"

He would not ask mamma. How cross he had been to her! He leaned against the wall to think. At last he looked up. "I know what I shall do with it!" he cried, and he started down the stairs.

Johnny carried it to the river, and threw it far out into the water. The heavy thing sank down, down, into the mud and slime. Johnny's heart was growing lighter all the time that it was sinking. "I can make a pretty bubble now!" he cried. He ran gayly to the garret for his pipe.

O, that bubble that he blew, when he had thrown his bad thoughts from him! I wish you might have seen it as it floated in the air. Johnny could not tell, himself, as he blew, what he was making. When he stopped at last to look at it, his tears were those of joy. Upon the airy bubble a silver mist seemed parting, and an angel with white wings was smiling back at him. — *From " Twilight Stories," by Elizabeth E. Foulke.*

By permission of Silver, Burdett & Company, publishers.

LESSON XX.

JOSEPH THE RULER.

"See I have set thee over all the land of Egypt." — Gen. 41 : 41.

WHEN the band of Midianites, to whom his brothers had sold Joseph, reached Egypt, they sold him to a man named Potiphar. Joseph's life now was very different from the life he had led at home. His father had always been kind and loving to him; here in Potiphar's house he was only a servant. Joseph tried to do what was right, however, and he served Potiphar so faithfully, and was always so kind and cheerful, that after a time Potiphar made him ruler over the rest of the servants in his house; that is, the other servants were all told to do whatever Joseph said. Still, Joseph could not be as happy as he would have been in his own home; but God planned it all, and you will see that it was all for the best.

After a time some one told Potiphar a wicked lie about Joseph. Potiphar was so angry that, without waiting to learn whether it was really true, he put Joseph in prison. Even in the prison God blessed Joseph, and, because he always did what was right, the keeper of the prison gave him charge over the other prisoners. This made it much easier for him, and he was thankful to God for helping him.

When Joseph had been in prison several years, King Pharaoh dreamed two dreams that were so strange that he wanted to know what they meant. There were people in Egypt who said that they could tell the meaning of dreams. The king told them his dream and asked the meaning, but they could not tell him. Pharaoh was very angry with them. At last some one told the king about Joseph, and that perhaps he could tell what was the meaning of the dreams. The king sent for Joseph to be brought out of prison to him.

When Joseph came before Pharaoh, the king said, "I have dreamed a dream, and there is none that can interpret it: and I have heard say of thee, that when thou hearest a dream thou canst interpret it." And Joseph answered Pharaoh, saying, "It is not in me: God shall give Pharaoh an answer of peace." Joseph did not wish Pharaoh to think that he could tell what the dream meant; only God could do that, but God could make the dream plain to Joseph, and Joseph could tell Pharaoh.

Then the king told his dream. He said that he thought he stood by a river, and that seven good-looking cattle were eating the grass by the river's side. Then seven other cattle, which were thin and bad-looking, came up out of the river and ate up the seven fat cattle. Then Pharaoh awoke, but he soon fell asleep and dreamed again. This time he thought he saw seven ears of corn growing on one stalk, and they were ripe and good; but after them came seven other ears of corn that were blasted by the wind and were thin and poor-looking. In his dream Pharaoh thought that the poor ears of corn ate up the seven good ears of corn.

God showed Joseph what the dream meant; and Joseph told Pharaoh that the dreams meant the same thing, and that he had had the two dreams because God wished to show him that they would surely come true. Joseph told the king that the seven fat cattle and the seven good ears of corn meant seven years when there should be plenty to eat. Then after this there would be seven years when nothing would grow and there would be no food, and they would be like the seven ears of corn that were bad and blasted. Joseph told Pharaoh that it would be best to find some one who was very wise to take charge of the food through the seven years of plenty, so that there should be some food kept for the years when nothing would grow.

Pharaoh was very much pleased to learn what the dreams meant. He said that he knew of no one as wise as Joseph, and he made him ruler over all Egypt. The king took a gold ring off his finger, and put it upon Joseph's hand. He dressed him in a beautiful robe of linen, and put a chain of gold about his neck.

Then Joseph ordered that a part of the corn and other grain which was raised during the year be put into great barns to keep until the years when there should be no food. Each year Joseph did this, until he had to have new barns built to hold all the grain.

One especial thing we want to remember about this lesson of Joseph is that God made it all for the best. Even the selling of Joseph to be a slave far from his home was really a good thing for Joseph, because in that way he became a great man in Egypt, second only to the king. Another time we shall see how it was a good thing for the others. God makes everything work together for good.

MEMORY GEM.

And suppose the world don't please you,
   Nor the way some people do;
Do you think the whole creation
   Will be altered just for you?
And is n't it, my boy or girl,
   The wisest, bravest plan,
Whatever comes or does n't come,
   To do the best you can?

OCCUPATION.

Build with the blocks Pharaoh's throne, and place on this something to represent the king. Let Joseph be brought in, the dream told, and the interpretation; then let Pharaoh give to Joseph the ring and royal robe as insignia of his new office.

STORY.—SULKY SIBYL.

There was no help for it; their visit to the pantomime must be delayed. The rain was coming down in torrents, and Aunt Sophy was up-stairs with one of her terrible headaches. But, had it been ever so fine, she could not have taken them. Of course, it was very disappointing, for they were to have had such a lovely time! Grandmamma was to have met them afterward, and driven them home to have supper with her, as it was Sibyl's birthday.

"Well," cried Eric, "we must amuse ourselves somehow. Perhaps it will be for the best. Besides, auntie says she will take us another day."

"But it won't be my birthday," argued Sibyl, with a shrug of her pretty shoulders. "It's horrid staying indoors on one's birthday, with nothing nice to do."

"Suppose you make auntie a cup of tea your very own self," suggested Mary, the peacemaker of the family. "You know she thinks so much of our waiting on her when she is ill."

"Indeed I shall not," said Sibyl, haughtily. "Jane can do that. Besides, I think she could have gone, had she liked."

"O Sibyl!" cried the brothers and sisters, reproachfully.

Now Sibyl intended, when she got up that morning, to have so happy a day! It began well enough.

Certainly the Indian mail had not come with the letter from papa and mamma, who never forgot them on their birthdays; but then there was the locket from grandmamma, and a purse from Aunt Sophy. Eric had given her a story-book she had been longing to read, and Mary and Norah must have spent all their pocket-money on a beautiful little box. Sibyl should have been the happiest of little girls; but unfortunately she could not bear not to have her own way. So, while Mary, Eric, and Norah prepared tea and toast to take up to Aunt Sophy, Sibyl stood by with a frown on her pretty face, and an ugly feeling in her heart. It was of no use coaxing; they all knew poor Sibyl was "in one of her sulks," as the family termed it; the only thing to be done was to take no notice.

So Sibyl sulked and sulked, and made every one miserable around her, and would most likely have kept up her sulky fit until the next morning, had not a big knock at the hall door and a tremendous ring at the bell startled her out of it.

"A telegram from father, to wish you a happy birthday," cried Eric, dancing into the room, holding a telegram addressed to Aunt Sophy, in his hand.

"Sibyl! Sibyl! Such a surprise!" he exclaimed, a minute afterward as he again rushed into the room. "Hurrah! Hurrah! Father and mother are coming home. They have left the ship, and will be here in less than an hour! What now about missing the pantomime, Miss Sibyl? Did n't I say it was all for the best?"—*Dutton's Holiday Annual.*

LESSON XXI.

IOSEPH AND HIS BRETHREN.

" Be ye kind one to another, tenderhearted, forgiving each other, even as God also in Christ forgave you." — Eph. 4 : 32.

THERE was a famine in Canaan where Joseph's father, Jacob, lived; and, when he heard that there was corn in Egypt, he sent Joseph's ten brothers there after corn. He kept Benjamin, the youngest, at home, for he was afraid that some harm would come to him. Neither Jacob nor his sons knew that Joseph had become the governor of Egypt; and, when the brothers saw him, they did not know him. He was a boy when they sold him to the Ishmaelites; now he was a man. Joseph knew his brothers, but he did not wish to have them know him at first. He wanted to see whether they were sorry because they had treated him so unkindly years before.

As Joseph was the governor of Egypt, when his brothers came to him, they bowed down to him and called him "my lord," and said they were his servants. You see how exactly the dream came true. Joseph asked them about their home, about their father and their families. They supposed he was an Egyptian, for he spoke in that language. They could not understand it, and a man stood by who told them in their own language what Joseph said. His brothers thought that he could not understand them; so they talked among themselves, and from what they said Joseph thought they were really sorry they had been so wicked to him when he was a boy.

Still, Joseph did not tell them who he was; he

wanted to be very sure that they were truly sorry. He asked them about their younger brother Benjamin, and said that they must bring him down to Egypt that he might see whether they were telling the truth. Finally he gave them the corn, and they went back to Canaan, and told Jacob all that the governor had said and done. When Jacob learned that the governor had told them not to come again after more corn unless they brought Benjamin with them, he felt sad. He had missed Joseph so much, and Benjamin was his youngest son and so dearly loved that he was afraid something would happen to him if he, too, went down to Egypt.

At length, however, their corn was all gone and the brothers must go to Egypt for more. They told their father they did not dare to go without Benjamin, for the governor had said he must come. At last Jacob let him go with his brothers. When Joseph heard that his brothers had returned to Egypt, he ordered a fine dinner, and invited them all to his house, as he was going to have them dine with him.

The brothers did not know what was going to happen to them because they were taken to the governor's own house. They bowed themselves to the earth, and had a present ready to give him. Joseph spoke to them kindly, and asked them whether their father was well. When he saw Benjamin, he was so glad that he could not keep the tears back, and he went into his chamber that the brothers might not see him weep. He was not ready to tell them who he was yet. When he came to seat them at dinner, he placed the oldest first and then the rest in the order of their ages; and they wondered how the Egyptian governor knew so much about them.

After Joseph had talked more with them he felt sure that they were really sorry for their wrongdoing. He told all the servants to leave the room;

and, when only he and his brothers were left, he told them who he was, and kissed them. He was very kind to them, and told them not to grieve because they had sold him away into Egypt. God had sent him there to tell the king of the famine that was to come, and to save the corn from other years for this time when there would be none. Then he also told them to go back to their home and tell his father that he was well and happy in Egypt. He sent wagons to bring his father and all his household down to Egypt to live near him.

When the brothers returned to Canaan and told their father all that Joseph had said, he was very much pleased, and hastened to gather all his things together and go to Egypt. How happy a man he was when he reached Egypt and saw all his sons together, and found Joseph, whom he loved and had missed so much, governor of Egypt!

Joseph took his father to the king's house, and Jacob blessed Pharaoh; and the king gave him all the land of Goshen in which to live. So Jacob and his sons and all their families lived there, and tended their cattle. Thus we see how God could make even so wicked an act as selling their own brother to be a slave, come out right in the end, and how he could make it a blessing, not only to the brothers and their father, but also to all the people of Egypt, for without Joseph they would have had no food.

God brought good out of the evil that the brothers did; but their wrong-doing hurt them, and they could never be as happy, because they must always remember how wicked they had been.

MEMORY GEM.

O, many a shaft at random sent
Finds mark the archer little meant!

And many a word at random spoken
May soothe or wound a heart that's broken.
— *Sir Walter Scott.*

OCCUPATION.

Carry out the idea of the lesson by having the brothers go down to Egypt for corn, and finally Jacob and all his family make the journey. This can be made more or less elaborate as desired. Cardboard can be used for tents. Cattle and servants may be represented or not as desired.

STORY.— THE HITCHING-POST.

"Harry!" called his father, "I have something new to show you. See this smooth, straight post. I am going to have Tom put this into the ground in front of the house so that the horses may be hitched to it. You are so fond of tying the horses that I thought I would let the post be yours. I am always pleased to see my boy show himself a little gentleman, as he does when he offers to hold or hitch their horses for our friends; but it grieves me when he is not just as polite and kind to his own little brother."

Harry hung his head, for he had just taken away the shovel from his younger brother, Roger, to use himself.

"The post is yours, Harry; but, when you say an unkind word to Roger, or do to him what you would not like to have him do to you, then I shall have to drive a nail into the post to remind you that you were unkind. Then, whenever you show yourself kind and unselfish, I will draw one out."

For several days Harry was very careful to do what would please Roger, but after that he forgot and spoke to him in so unkind a way that his father was much grieved. Taking Harry by the hand, he went out to the post, and a nail was driven part way into the wood.

Harry determined that the nail should soon come out, for he intended to be very kind to Roger. The next day it rained so hard that Roger could not go out-of-doors to play, and Harry offered to stay in the house with him. That night, when his father came home and asked about the day, he told Harry that they would pull out that nail. Harry had been almost ready to cry when it was driven into his post, but now he felt very happy, and said to himself that no more nails would need to be driven. The next day, however, Harry was careless and did not try to be unselfish to his brother, and that night two nails were driven into the post. These stayed in, and others soon followed them.

Then Harry grew naughty about it, and said to himself: "I don't care if father does drive the nails into the post. I can't help it anyway."

Some time after this, as Harry stood under the open sitting-room window late one afternoon, he overheard Roger say: "O papa, please do not drive the nail into the post. I don't think Harry meant to spoil my play, and perhaps he will do better tomorrow."

Harry wandered round to the front of the house and looked at the hitching-post; then he counted the nails and thought about what Roger had just said. He began to feel ashamed of himself. "It is too bad to be unkind to such a dear, good brother. What a lot of nails father has had to drive in!" Harry began to reckon to see how long it would take him to get all the nails out again if his father drew out two a day. He stood looking at the post for some time, and at last said to himself, "I will do better, and if possible two of those nails shall come out each day until they are all gone."

Harry did try. He worked hard to please Roger, and nail after nail was drawn out. Sometimes he failed, and only one nail could be taken out at night; once in a while another nail was driven in; but most of the time Harry succeeded so well in doing to Roger just as he would have liked to have Roger do to him, that the nails were fast disappearing from the post, and all the family spoke of how pleasant Harry was growing.

At last came the day when there was but one nail left, and Harry and his father went out to the post to draw out that one. As Harry watched his father take it out, the tears began to gather in his eyes; and soon he could not bear it any longer, but began to cry outright.

"Why, what's the matter, Harry?" asked his father. "I thought you would be glad to have the nails all out."

"I am glad, father; but the holes are still there, and I can't help thinking how many times I must have done wrong to make so many nail-holes."

"That is the sad part of it, my son. Wrong-doing does leave a scar that we can never remove. We must always bear the mark of it upon ourselves; but God is sorry for us when we do wrong, and is always ready to forgive us and help us if we truly wish to do better."

LESSON XXII.

MOSES.

"Thus did Moses: according to all that the Lord commanded him, so did he." — Exod. 40: 16.

ONE day a king's daughter went to the river to bathe. When she and her maidens reached the place, they saw a basket out in the water. She sent one of her maidens to bring it to the shore. When the princess looked inside, there lay a dear little baby, who looked up into her face and began to cry. She pitied the poor little thing. He was so sweet that she wanted to kiss him and love him.

Should you like to know why this little baby was out in the water in the curious basket? We shall have to think back to the time when Joseph had all his brothers come from Canaan to Egypt to live. You remember there were eleven of them. They all had sons and daughters, and these had children until by and by they became a great nation just as God had promised Abraham, and were called "the children of Israel."

After a time there was another king who did not remember Joseph or the good he had done. This king began to be unkind to God's people and to make them work very hard. Then he grew cruel, and treated them so badly that they were afraid of him. This wicked king would even hurt little boys. One mother who had a dear boy baby was so afraid that something would happen to him that she hid

FINDING OF MOSES.
From a painting by Delaroche.

him in the house until he grew so large that she feared some one would hear him cry. She was afraid whenever any one came near the house, for fear the dear little baby boy would be hurt. At last she made a basket like a boat of bulrushes, and covered the outside of it with slime and pitch, so that the water would not get inside. When it was all done, she placed the little babe in the basket, and, carrying it down by the river Nile, she left it among the reeds that grew by the bank.

I know you will understand how hard it was for her to put her dear little baby out there in the water, but she was doing the best she could that nothing should hurt her little one. She left his older sister by the bank of the river to watch and see whether all was right.

Then the daughter of the king came to the river to bathe, and found the basket boat with its sweet babe. As she stood there looking down at the little face, the baby's sister, Miriam, who had been watching all the time, came to her side. I am sure Miriam was a little afraid, for she had never spoken to a princess, but she must do what she could for her dear brother. So she asked the king's daughter whether she would like to have her find a nurse to take care of the babe. The princess told her she might go for one, and Miriam ran home and brought her mother. When she came, the princess told her that, if she would take the child and nurse him, she would pay her good wages.

Miriam and the mother hastened home with the baby, very happy, for now no one would hurt him. The princess had asked the woman to take care of the babe, and no one would dare do anything to a child that belonged to the king's daughter.

The mother taught him about the God who made him and made all the things he saw around him.

She taught him to do what God said, whether it was easy or not. When he grew older, his mother took him to the king's palace, where he lived with the princess as if he were her own son. She called him Moses, and had the wise men of the land teach him all that they could. Thus he became a wise and good man, for he did not forget what his own mother had taught him about God and about serving him. After a number of years God told Moses that he wished him to go to the king and ask him to let his people, the children of Israel, go away from Egypt back to Canaan, and God promised to help Moses. Then Moses did whatever the Lord said, and God helped him as he had promised.

MEMORY GEM.

Two little eyes to look to God,
Two little ears to hear his word,
One little tongue to speak his truth,
One heart to give him now in my youth,
Two little feet to walk his ways,
Two hands to work for him all my days;
Take them, dear Jesus, and may they be
Ever obedient and true to thee.

OCCUPATION.

A rough representation of the ark of bulrushes can easily be made by weaving together splints, or even by cutting strips from stiff paper. Make the river and the bank on the sand-board, and place the ark in the river. Place the figure to represent Miriam near by; and, when the princess and her maidens come, let one of them draw the ark to the shore. Then Miriam should be sent to bring the mother.

STORY.—JUST AS WELL.

"Be sure, my child," said the widow to her little daughter, "that you always do just as you are told."

"Very well, mother."

"Or, at any rate, do what will do just as well," said the small house-dog, called So-so, as he lay blinking at the fire.

One day the widow was going out on business, and she called her little daughter, and said to her: "I am going out for two hours. You are too young to protect yourself and the house, and So-so is not as strong as Faithful was. But, when I go, shut the house-door, and bolt the big wooden bar, and be sure that you do not open it for any reason whatever till I return. If strangers come, So-so may bark, which he can do as well as a bigger dog. Then they will go away. With this summer's savings I have bought a quilted petticoat for you and a duffle cloak for myself for winter; and, if I get the work I am going after to-day, I shall buy enough wool to knit warm stockings for both of us. So be patient till I return, and then we will have the plum-cake that is in the cupboard for tea."

"Thank you, mother."

"Good-by, my child. Be sure to do just as I have told you," said the widow.

"Very well, mother."

Little Joan laid down her doll, and shut the house-door, and fastened the big bolt. It was very heavy, and the kitchen looked gloomy when she had done it. She got into the rocking-chair to put her doll to sleep. After a time she grew tired of this.

"It's a beautiful day," said little Joan. "I wish mother had allowed us to sit on the door-step. We could have taken care of the house —"

"Just as well," said So-so. "The air smells fresh," he continued.

Little Joan came to smell the air at the keyhole, and, as So-so had said, it smelt very fresh. Besides, one could see from the window how fine the evening was.

"It's not exactly what mother told us to do," said Joan, "but I do believe —"

"It would do just as well," said So-so.

By and by little Joan unfastened the bar and opened the door, and she and the doll and So-so went out and sat on the door-step.

"It does just as well, and better," said little Joan; "for, if any one comes, we can see him coming up the field path."

"Just so," said So-so, blinking in the sunshine.

Suddenly Joan jumped up. "O!" cried she, "there's a bird, a big bird. Dear So-so, can you see him?"

"I'll catch him," said So-so, and he put up his tail and started off.

"No, no!" cried Joan. "You must stay and take care of the house, and bark if any one comes."

While they were talking, an old woman came up to the door; she had a brown face, and black hair, and a very old red cloak.

"Good evening, my little dear," said she. "Are you all at home this fine evening?"

"Only three of us," said Joan, "I, and my doll, and So-so. Mother has gone to the town on business, and we are taking care of the house; but So-so wants to go after the bird we saw run into the corn. I should like to go after it myself, but we can't leave the house."

"I have some distance to go this evening," said the old woman, "but I do not object to a few minutes' rest; and sooner than that you should lose the bird I will sit on the door-step to oblige you, while you run down to the corn-field."

They did not catch the bird, though they stayed longer than they had intended. When they reached the house, the old woman had gone, and she had taken the quilted petticoat and the duffle cloak, and the plum-cake from the top shelf, away with her, and was never seen again.

When the widow reached home and found what had happened, she felt very sad; for she did not know where she could get more clothes to take the place of the ones the old woman had stolen, and, what was worse, her daughter had not obeyed and done what her mother had said.

"For the future, my child," said the widow, "I hope you will always do just as you are told, whatever So-so may say." — *Arranged from Mrs. Juliana Horatia Ewing.*

LESSON XXIII.

THE WILDERNESS.

"I will rain bread from heaven . . . that I may prove them, whether they will walk in my law or no." — *Exod. 16: 4.*

GOD had made King Pharaoh let the children of Israel go away from Egypt. God had helped Moses in all that he had to do, just as he had promised. Now the people were to be taken through a great wilderness in order to get to the promised land of Canaan. Do you know what this wilderness was like? It was not a beautiful country with green grass and trees, with streets and houses, or with great fields of corn and grain. The ground was hot and sandy. It was a dreary place.

The Israelites had carried water with them from Egypt, but after a time this was gone and they grew thirsty. By and by they came to some water, but it was bitter and not good to drink. The people were very much disappointed, and complained and scolded about it just as children do when things do not please them. But God loved his people. He did not wish them to suffer; he longed to have them feel that he would care for them, just as he wishes us to know that he will do for us whatever is best. God taught Moses how to make the water fit to drink. How glad they were to have plenty of good water after being so thirsty! Should you think that they would forget how kind God had been to them?

The diffcrent kinds of grain — corn, wheat, and barley — did not grow in the wilderness; and the

Israelites had soon eaten all their food and begun to be hungry. No animals lived there that could be caught and used for food. The people thought of the time when they lived in Egypt and had plenty to eat, but they thought little about all the work they had been obliged to do. They also forgot how God had made the bitter water sweet. Instead of asking him to help them, they complained because Moses had brought them away from Egypt, where there was corn and grain.

God had not taken his people from a country where there was plenty of food to starve them in the wilderness. The children of Israel were his chosen people. He loved them and would take care of them; but he wished them to do just what he said, to trust and obey. When the Israelites complained because they had not enough to eat, God made a great flock of quail fly down near the ground. There were a great many of these birds, and they had been flying so far and were so tired that they were easily caught. The people captured a great many of them, not only enough for them to eat at the time, but many more, which they preserved so that they had plenty of meat for some time.

The next morning, when the children of Israel awoke, the ground was covered with a white, frost-like thing that they had never seen before. It seemed as if it had rained down from heaven. It lay all over the ground like frost in the early morning. The people did not know what to make of it. God had told them that it was for food; so some of the people ground it fine, and made it into a kind of bread that was sweet and good when baked. The people called this white thing "manna," and after a little time all the people gathered it to cook and eat.

God told the people to gather enough for one day, for he would send it to them fresh each morning,

Some of the people, however, took enough for more than one day; but in the morning they found the manna which they had not used was no longer good. However, the ground was covered with fresh manna as God had promised.

God wished them to rest from work on the seventh day, so as to have time to learn about him. Therefore the people were told to gather twice as much as usual on the sixth day, that they might have enough for the seventh day, which was called the "Sabbath," God's holy day. Some did not gather extra manna on the sixth day, thinking that they would find plenty on the next, although God had told them that they would not. When the morning of the Sabbath came, there was none to be found. The food gathered on the sixth day to be used on the Sabbath kept quite good, for God wished it to be so.

The people began to learn that it was better to do just as God said. They forgot this very often, but God was kind and forgave them, and cared for them all the time that they were in the wilderness. He cares for us now just as much as he did for the children of Israel, and it is right and best for us to do whatever God says, just as it was for them.

MEMORY GEM..

Over and over again,
  No matter which way I turn,
I always find in the book of life
  Some lesson I have to learn.

OCCUPATION.

Make cardboard tents to illustrate the habitations of the people. Scatter white seeds or grain to represent the manna which is to be gathered. Let the children think of themselves as the Israelites for the time being. A double portion of the manna should be gathered to last over the Sabbath.

STORY.—THE DAISY DANCE.

"Stella! Stella! Star! Star! Star!"

"Yes, here I am; I'm Stella, but who are you?"

"Just turn your head a little bit this way, and you'll see. How do you do, Stella, Star, Star?"

O, such a wee little bit of a lady! Perched right on the edge of a daisy, nodding away, as friendly as if she were a little grandma. Her little skirts stood out like wings, and her golden hair waved back from her pretty face. There were butterfly wings at her cunning shoulders.

"It isn't everybody that can see me. O, no; I only come to little people in their sleep, and then, when they wake up, they know they've had a dream; but they remember what I've told them, because I'm really a little spirit of the air, a fairy, if you like. I heard you sigh because there were no children just your age for you to play with. But you're just in time for a daisy dance. And such fun! If there are any questions you want to ask, you can, and I'll try to answer, but you had better ask before the dance begins!"

"Then, pretty fairy, what made you call me Star?"

"Because I heard them call you Stella, and Stella means star."

"And please what is a daisy dance?"

"That you'll see in a moment, Stella, Star. We fairies love everything sweet and bright. That is why I like to call you Star, because the stars with their twinkling eyes are always dear friends to the fairies. But see; here comes our merry brother,

Breeze, and all the Daisy family are up and finely dressed, all ready for their promised dance. Look now! One! two! three! and go!"

O, what a sight! All over the daisy meadow fine little daisy queens and smart little daisy princes bowing to each other, then courtesying and nodding; up and down in rows and rows they flew toward each other, then back again, their white dresses and yellow belts hiding their little green stockings as they swayed back and forth, keeping time to the wild, sweet music of the fairy's brother Breeze.

"Do they dance every day?" asked Stella.

"No; sometimes it rains, and then my sisters tuck their delicate dresses about their yellow belts, and stand quietly in the grass which shelters them. There they stand until told what next to do."

"Why, do such little things as daisies learn what they must do?"

"Certainly, Stella, Star. I am the Queen of the Summer, and we have our laws just as much as your mother has her little laws or rules that you must obey."

"But suppose a daisy won't obey; what then?"

"Then the poor little thing withers away. I am always sorry. But, queen though I am, I cannot keep a daisy alive that will not obey daisy laws."

"But I thought daisies were just daisies," said Stella. "I thought they happened to spring up, and lived a little while, only for the reason that they happened to live. I did n't know there was any use for them, but thought they soon happened to die, just as they had happened to live."

"O my dear Stella, Star! Nothing only happens in the world. I don't know why this is, because I 'm only a little sprite of the air. But long ago I found out there were laws, very kind and gentle ones, yet laws for everything that is ever made, even for the stones. Nearly every daisy that grows is good and obedient; but once in a while — O, dear! Perhaps you'll understand best if I tell you about a daisy that would not obey. When the sun begins to shut his great red eye, I cry, 'Come, daisies all, hold up your mouths for your supper. Here it comes, soft, sweet, gentle dew; take all you can.' But naughty daisy would n't hold up her head, would n't open her mouth, would n't obey a word. Pretty soon I called, 'Come, daisies all, fold your dresses close, and shut up your bright little eyes; night has come; it is time to sleep.' But this naughty little daisy kept her eyes wide open and her delicate dress unfolded. Early in the dewy morning I called again: 'Come, daisies all, morning is here; spread your white dresses and drink in the drops, the cool, refreshing drops falling from the sky and sparkling with the rays of the sun.' But naughty daisy would not drink, would not look up, would not obey. At noon, when the sun grew hot, and the bees were humming about, and the birds were fairly shaking with song, poor little daisy began to droop. Her pretty dress hung straight down, leaving her yellow belt standing alone and bare. Her merry friends, the bees, knew there was no honey in her deep little heart; the birds knew there was no use to sing her a song. I would gladly have helped poor foolish little daisy, if I could; but not even a daisy can live if it breaks the laws that are made for its life. So she drooped and fell. And her little brothers and sisters spread their white dresses over the place where she lay, and she was seen no more." — *From " The Fairies of Fern Dingle," by Harriet A. Cheever. Congregational Publishing Society.*

LESSON XXIV.

THE TEN COMMANDMENTS.

" Thou shalt love the Lord thy God with all thy heart, and with all thy soul, and with all thy mind. . . . Thou shalt love thy neighbor as thyself." — *Matt. 22 : 37, 39.*

WHEN the children of Israel had been three months in the wilderness, they came to the mountain called Sinai. Here God told them to rest awhile. They put up their tents and stayed a number of weeks, for God had a great many things to tell them and many wonders to show them. Moses went up the mountain to talk with God, but the people stayed at the foot. God told Moses to speak to the people; to remind them how he had brought them from Egypt, how he had made the water good to drink, how he had given them food, and how he had cared for them all the way. Then God promised to take care of them always, and that they should become a great nation, his own chosen people, if they would obey him. And all the people promised to do whatever God said. He will do the same for us if we obey him.

Moses told the people that they must not go near the mountain, because God was coming down in his glory upon the mountain. No person but Moses must see God. A cloud hung over Mount Sinai, and it looked to the children of Israel as if it were on fire, and the whole mountain shook. Do you suppose Moses was afraid? He no doubt felt very solemn, but I do not think he was afraid. When he heard the trumpet of God, which sounded long and loud, he went up the mountain into the very midst of the cloud and smoke, and there he talked with God. He must have been a very holy man, for no one else has been allowed to speak with God in just this way.

God gave Moses ten commandments, ten laws that the people were to obey, just as many as there are fingers and thumbs on your two hands. They were written on two tables of stone by the finger of God himself. Moses stayed on the mountain with God forty days and forty nights, for there were many things that God wished to tell him. All this time the people of Israel stood away from the mountain, and saw the lightnings and the mountain smoking, and heard the thunderings and the noise of the trumpet.

The ten commandments that God gave the children of Israel are meant for us as much as for them. Let us use our two hands to help us remember about them. The first four commandments tell us how we ought to love and serve God. Let us begin with the thumb on the right hand. God said, "Thou shalt have none other gods before me." The people in Egypt thought there were many gods; there is but one. We are to have no other gods at all, for there is but one God. We must love him and try to do what will please him. We will remember for the thumb, "One God." The second commandment tells us *how* to worship God, and that, if we do as he wishes, he will bless us and all our children. For the pointer we will try to remember, "Worship God" in the right way. The third commandment says, "Thou shalt not take the name of the Lord thy God in vain." We must not use God's name in a careless way; we must not speak his name in fun or in a naughty way, but always remember that he is *God.* For the tall man we will remember that we must be reverent when we speak of God, and not laugh or play. The fourth commandment is, "Remember the Sabbath day, to keep it holy." God says we have six days in which to work and play, and the Sabbath day is for us to learn about him and to worship him.

Four commands God gave us about loving him; first, have but one God; second, worship him aright; third, speak of him in the right way; fourth, keep the Sabbath holy.

God has given us fathers and mothers to care for us, to teach us what is right to do, to help us do what will please God. We cannot see God; we do not understand about him as well as we do about father and mother. How kind and loving of God to give us our parents that we may learn how much God loves us by seeing how much our fathers and mothers love us! God has made our parents wiser than we, that they may tell us what to do; and he wishes us to obey them. The fifth commandment we will put for the little finger, next to the commands about loving God, "Honor thy father and thy mother." That is, love and obey them, and be kind and gentle to them, and always look up to them.

We will not take each of the other five separately, because it would be hard for you to remember them. They teach us to be kind and unselfish and loving to all. Jesus said to love God with all our heart, and to love those about us as we love ourselves. If we do this, we are keeping the ten commandments.

MEMORY GEM.

The Story of the "Forget-me-not."

When to flowers so beautiful
  The Father gave a name,
Back came a little blue-eyed one, —
  All timidly it came, —

And, standing at the Father's feet
  And gazing in his face,
It said with a meek and timid voice,
  Yet with a gentle grace,
" Dear Lord, the name thou gavest me,
  Alas ! I have forgot."
The Father kindly looked him down,
  And said, " Forget-me-not."
                    — *From the German.*

OCCUPATION.

Make Mount Sinai by the use of a crumpled sheet of tissue-paper. Have cardboard tents placed all about near the mountain. Mark off the line about the mountain, beyond which the Israelites were not to go. Let one figure go up the mountain alone. While Moses is hidden from view on the mountain, make vivid to the children the smoking mountain, the thunderings and shakings. When Moses descends, have ready a paper marked to represent the two tables of stone, with four figures in a column on one table and the other six on the other table. Let the children tell over the commandments as given for the right hand in the lesson ; for the left hand impress upon their minds the substance of the Golden Rule, doing as one would be done by.

STORY.—WHICH LOVED BEST?

"I love you, mother," said little John ;
Then, forgetting his work, his cap went on
And he was off to the garden swing,
And left her the water and wood to bring.

"I love you, mother," said rosy Nell,
" Love you better than tongue can tell."

Then she teased and pouted full half the day,
Till her mother rejoiced when she went to play.

"I love you, mother," said little Fan;
"To-day I'll help you all I can.
How glad I am that school does n't keep!"
So she rocked the baby till it fell asleep;

Then, stepping softly, she brought the broom,
And swept the floor and dusted the room;
Busy and happy all day was she,
Helpful and happy as child could be.

"I love you, mother," again they said,
Three little children going to bed.
Do you suppose that mother guessed
Which of them really loved her best?
—*Joy Allison.*

(Tell the story of the "Forget-me-not" to illustrate the first four commandments.)

LESSON XXV.

THE TABERNACLE.

"Ye shall keep my sabbaths, and reverence my sanctuary: I am the Lord."— Lev. 19: 30.

AFTER God had given Moses the ten commandments he told him that he wished the people to make a tabernacle in which they could worship him. As the children of Israel kept moving from place to place, they could not build anything like our churches; but they could have a large tent for God's house. God told Moses to build the tabernacle so that it could be taken to pieces when the children of Israel moved on to another place in the wilderness. It had two parts or rooms, one of them called the "holy of holies," where only Moses and Aaron could go.

A chest was made, covered with beautiful figures of leaves and flowers of pure gold. At each corner was a ring of solid gold. Through these rings were long poles covered with gold, by which the chest was carried. On the top were placed two lovely cherubs made of gold, with their wings spread over it. This chest was called the "ark of the covenant." In it were put the two tables of stone upon which God had written the ten commandments. The ark was placed in the inner room, the holy of holies; and in front of it hung an elegantly embroidered curtain, behind which the people were never to go.

God also told Moses what to make for the larger

room of the tabernacle. There was to be a table of showbread; this was also covered with gold, and on it stood two dishes upon which each Sabbath were placed twelve fresh loaves of bread. This table was to teach the people to love their homes. God wished them to love their homes, just as he wishes us to care for ours now.

A beautiful candlestick made of gold and having seven lights was to be kept burning all the time. God made the light that we have, the sunlight, the moonlight, and the light from the stars; even the lights we burn in our houses God got ready for us; so the light from the candlestick was to remind the people of God's kindness.

A golden altar was made, upon which incense was to be burned. When the priests offered incense, making sweet odors, the people prayed.

God told Moses to have beautiful curtains for the tabernacle. Some of them were to be embroidered with blue, scarlet, and purple.

A tent was made of goats' hair, over which were put other skins to protect all from the rain. Everything was of the best, for it was God's house.

Around the tent under which was the tabernacle was a court, into which the people were allowed to come. Even this court had curtains embroidered with different colors and gold. It was all made as beautiful as possible.

When the tabernacle was finished, a cloud covered the part where the ark stood. All the people could see this; even the women and children who might be some distance away from the tabernacle, tending their flocks in some spot where grass grew, could see the cloudy pillar and know just where the tabernacle stood. At night this cloud looked like fire, and could be seen all around.

Whenever God wished the people to go forward,

the cloud rose higher and moved on to the place where they were again to rest and pitch their tents. As long as the cloud remained over the tabernacle the children of Israel rested. When they were again to go forward, the cloud went before them. Thus the people knew when to remain in their tents and when to march on toward Canaan.

Thus God took care of his children all the time, though the children of Israel often did wrong. God forgave them a great many times, just as he does when we do wrong now. He wanted to help them as he is glad to help us now. He had them make the tabernacle for a holy place to him, that it might help them to remember him and all that he did for them. He wished them to pray to him there, and to reverence his house; to think it a holy, blessed place because it was his.

In just the same way God wishes us to think of his house, the church, as his home, a place where he is always ready to listen to us, where he is glad to have us go to worship and praise him and to learn about him. He is pleased when we go regularly to church, and when we try to sing and to understand what the minister is saying about Jesus. Even little children can please God by being quiet and listening in church.

MEMORY GEM.

> I was glad when they said unto me,
> Let us go unto the house of the Lord.
> Our feet are standing
> Within thy gates, O Jerusalem.
> — *Psalms.*

OCCUPATION.

There is a little model of the tabernacle that can be put together to show the different parts, the various hangings, the ark of the covenant, the candlestick, the table of showbread, etc. If this could be obtained, it would make the lesson very real and clear to the children. There are also paper illustrations of the tabernacle that the children can cut out and put together. If neither of these can be had, some picture of the tabernacle can be found as illustration, and it may be possible to find one that can be cut out and mounted so as to give a fair idea to the little ones.

STORY.—MAY AT CHURCH.

"Shall I dress May for church, mamma?" asked May's older sister Florence.

"I am afraid she can't go to-day, my daughter. My head aches so hard that I shall have to stay at home."

"O mamma! You said she might go if it was pleasant."

"Yes, I should be glad to take her if I could go; but you know she has never been to church, and I don't know how she would behave."

"I am sure she would be good with me, mamma. Could I take her? If I sat very still, I think she would."

"You are always a good girl at church, Florence, and May usually does whatever you do. Perhaps it would be safe to try her. When you have her dressed ready to go, bring her in here and I will talk with her. I want her to understand that she must be reverent in God's house."

Away flew Florence to find her little sister.

"O May! Mamma says you may go to church with me if you will be a good girl and do just as Florence does."

"I will, I will be good!"

Soon the two were dressed. Florence had combed and braided May's hair and tied it with a new blue ribbon. Then they went to their mother's room. Mamma saw that both the girls looked all right; then she said, as she laid her hand on her little girl's arm: "May is going to church for the first time. I want her to remember that she is in God's house, and that God himself is there, although she cannot see him. I hope she will remember that we go to church to worship God, to sing about him, to pray to him, and to listen to what the minister says about him. If we go with hearts full of love for God, and really want to show him that we know how great and good he is, we shall keep very quiet all the time we are in his house, and listen to all that is sung or said."

"Yes, mamma! I will sit as still as a mouse, and do just what Florence says."

Their mother watched the two children as they started down the country road, then darkened her room and lay down to see whether the pain in her head would be better.

Florence and May walked hand in hand along the shady road toward the village where they could see the church spire pointing to the beautiful sky, inviting all to look up at the beautiful trees, the fleecy clouds, and the lovely blue dome. A little bird was singing a sweet song, and seemed to keep just ahead of them as if to show them the way. Then the bell began to call softly and slowly. Soon they were in the cool, dark church out of the heat and glare of the sun. Everything was very quiet. May sat still, but looked about her. There were a great many people, more than she had ever seen together before. The church was plain, but to May it seemed very grand. She felt quiet, and wondered whether it was because God was so near.

Soon the choir began to sing. May loved music dearly, and would listen as long as any one sung. When the white-haired old man stood up in the pulpit and began to read slowly and clearly from the Bible, May looked up into his sweet face and wondered whether he looked so kind because he was in God's house so much. Then another hymn was sung, and again May was perfectly happy. As the others all bowed their heads in prayer, May did the same. It was still and quiet in the church, very different from the drowsy hum of the bees in the hot sunshine outside, or the bright, sunny rooms at home.

After a little the minister began to preach. It was a long sermon, and our little girl could not understand much of what the minister said. One sentence she remembered and thought about: "If we think of the song of the birds and the music of the brooks as praise offered to God, they will help us to true worship of him." May wondered whether that meant that the birds and the brooks went to church, too. On her way home she asked Florence about it.

"I don't know as he exactly meant that the birds go to church, but it seems to me that they sing to God because they are so glad, just as we sing at church because God has made us happy."

When they reached home, mamma knew by one look at their faces that May had been a good girl, and said, "Did my little one like the church?"

"O, yes, mamma! I liked it so much. The singing was so pretty, and the minister looked so kind. I hope I can go each Sunday now."

LESSON XXVI.

JOSHUA.

" These stones shall be for a memorial unto the children of Israel forever." — Josh. 4: 7.

The children of Israel had travelled about in the wilderness for many years, and they were anxious to reach the land that God had promised to give them. God had told them that it was a beautiful country, that a great many kinds of fruit and grain grew there, and that there was plenty of good water. God's people were tired of wandering from place to place, and wanted to have homes for themselves. The children hardly knew what it meant to have a home to come to when they had finished their play. They did not know how good it seems to get home again after being away for a few days.

Between the people and the good country, the land God had promised them, was a great river, the river Jordan. No bridge crossed the river, and the children of Israel had no boats. What should they do? Then God told Joshua that he would help them. He had been taking care of his people all the way, and he would show them how to cross the river.

Do you remember that Moses had made a beautiful ark covered with gold to stand in the tabernacle, and that in this ark were the tables of stone on which were written the ten commandments, and that this ark was holy because it was for God?

When the people wished to cross the river, God told Joshua to have the priests take up the ark of the covenant and go before them to the river. The people were told not to go too near the ark, because it was holy. The priests were directed to stand still when they reached the river. Then Joshua told the children of Israel that God had taken care of them all the way, and that he would help them to cross the river. The priests stepped into the water, and all the people watched to see whether God would keep his promise and provide a way for them to cross. Should you not think they would have remembered how God had given them food and water in the wilderness and how he had helped them all the way, and believe that he would do as he promised?

God always keeps his promises, and he did this time. God promised that as soon as the feet of the priests who carried the ark should touch the water, the river would stop flowing and the water stand up in a pile, and then the people could go across on dry ground. Think of the water of some river near your home piling up in a heap at one side for you to walk across. We can hardly imagine such a thing as happening. But that is what God promised to do for his people.

As soon as the priests stepped into the water, the whole river was stopped above them, and the people walked across on dry ground. The priests stood still until all the people had gone over.

When all the nation had passed over the river Jordan, then the Lord spake unto Joshua, and told him to have twelve men go to the place where the priests had stood in the river, and to have each take a stone and carry it on his shoulder to the place where they stopped for the night, and there make a monument. Thus all should remember how God had stopped the water of the river Jordan that they might walk across.

After a time, when the little children grew larger

and asked what that pile of stones was for, then the parents answered, "Because the waters of Jordan were cut off before the ark of the covenant of the Lord, and these stones shall be for a memorial unto the children of Israel forever."

God was pleased to have his people tell of this, because he always wishes us to remember whenever he helps us, and to thank him for all the good times he gives us.

MEMORY GEM.

Butterflies and blossoms fair,
And bees and birds and brooks,
Sunshine sweet and summer air.
And silent, shady nooks, —
God just loves to let us play
In playgrounds where he lives.
O, won't we thank him every day
Who gives and gives and gives?
— *Selected.*

OCCUPATION.

Represent the river Jordan by two long strips of paper, and have in the bed of the river twelve or more blocks for the stones. Place the men on one side of the river. Have the priests carrying the ark walk down to the brook; and, as they touch the edge of the paper, move it back and double it up to represent the waters heaped up. Let the children move all the people across to the other side, and then select twelve men to go back to where the priests still stand with the ark, and bring the twelve stones and build the memorial. Then have the priests carry the ark across and the waters of the river return to their places.

STORY.—GOD WILL KNOW.

There is a beautiful story told of two little children standing in front of a handsomely lighted window in one of our large cities. In the window were displayed tempting cakes and candies, and luscious fruits of all kinds. The eyes of both children looked longingly at the holiday sweets; but the little girl, who was considerably older than her brother, soon felt the tears coming to her eyes, for she knew how impossible it was for them to have even a taste of the good things in the store. Even the little boy knew that there was no money with which to buy candy. As he continued to look at the fascinating things inside the window, he began to cry softly to himself.

"O Harry," said his sister, "don't cry. Wouldn't it be nice if we could carry home something to mamma? If you could have whatever you wanted, what would you choose?"

"That big orange," sighed Harry, as he bravely choked down his sobs. "Perhaps it would make her better."

"Is your mother sick, little girl?" asked a kind voice behind them.

"Yes, sir," she slowly answered; but, gaining courage from the pleasant smile on the man's face, she continued, "the doctor says she ought to have good things to eat, and we were only playing choose something for her."

"Suppose you come inside and choose," continued the gentleman, who had been watching the children and had overheard the conversation.

"But we have no money, sir," said the little girl, and again her eyes filled with tears.

"Come in with me, and we will see what can be done."

The children were delighted at the invitation, but

were too shy to do as he suggested. Taking them by the hand, he led them inside, and then bought more than they could carry of such good things as they had seen in the window. As they walked along, the little girl said, "Will you please tell me your name, sir?"

"O, never mind my name."

"But mamma has told me to always pray for those who are kind to me and my brother, and I should like to tell God who you are."

The gentleman looked very tenderly at the little girl, but only said, "Never mind about my name."

When they reached the place where the children lived, the gentleman laid his gifts on the door-step and turned away with a cheery "Good-by," but the little girl said, "Well, sir, if you won't tell me your name, when I tell God about your kindness to us, he will know who you are."

LESSON XXVII.

THE FALL OF JERICHO.

"*Suffer hardship with me, as a good soldier of Christ Jesus.*" — 2 Tim. 2:3.

THERE was a great city called Jericho, which the children of Israel wished to enter. All around the outside was a high wall so that no one could climb over. The gates were all closed, and no one who did not live there could get in, because the people did not wish the Israelites to come into their city. The people of Israel had put up their tents in front and were waiting, since they knew not what to do.

One day, as Joshua was thinking what could be done, the Lord talked with him and said that he would help the people, and that they should go into the city of Jericho. Then God told Joshua just what to do.

Joshua called the priests, and said, "Take up the ark of the covenant, and let seven priests bear seven trumpets of rams' horns before the ark of the Lord." Then Joshua told the men to march around the city ahead of the priests that carried the ark. Joshua told the people not to shout or to make any noise. They marched around the city, and the priests followed, carrying the ark and blowing the trumpets. When they had been around the city they went back to their tents for the night.

The next day they marched around the city in the same manner, the priests blowing the trumpets, but the rest of the people keeping quiet. Then they returned to their tents for the night. The third day they again marched around the city walls, and went again to their tents. On the fourth day and on the fifth day and on the sixth day they marched around the city.

"On the seventh day they rose early at the dawning of the day," and marched as on the other days except that this day they went around the city seven times instead of but once. During the seventh time the trumpets blew a loud blast, and "Joshua said unto the people, Shout; for the Lord hath given you the city. So the people shouted and the priests blew with the trumpets: and it came to pass, when the people heard the sound of the trumpet, that the people shouted with a great shout, and the wall fell down flat, so that the people went up into the city."

Thus God let his people go into the city because they did just what he told them to do, and because they believed he would do what he had promised. It must have seemed strange to God's people to be told to march around the city once each day for six days and seven times on the seventh day. God wished them to obey even if it did seem strange. We all must obey; we must obey God, we must obey our fathers and mothers, we must obey our teachers. Even the son of a king or the president must obey.

Sometimes you sing, "We are little soldiers." Then, if you are to be soldiers, you must obey those who have the rule over you. Soldiers do not ask, "Why?" but obey without a word. Soldiers do not stop to see whether what they are told to do will be pleasant, but they obey at once. Soldiers do not scowl when they are told to do something, but go about it with cheerful faces.

Let us see whether for one week we can obey like soldiers, without question or hesitation, but quickly and cheerfully.

MEMORY GEM.

I'm a little soldier
Of the heavenly King;
Ever in his praises
I can speak and sing.

OCCUPATION.

Build the city of Jericho, houses and city wall, taking pains to make the wall the proper height in proportion to the height of whatever is to be used to represent the men. Pitch the tents outside the city wall. March the men and priests once around the city, and have them return to the camp. Have the men who represent the priests carrying trumpets differ in some way from the other men, and have priests carry the ark. Let the children move the whole procession around the city in as orderly a manner as possible. This can easily be done by putting all the men on a sheet of paper, and gently sliding the paper along. The procession can be made to march around the city as many times as the teacher thinks best; but the children should be made to understand that it really went around once each day for six days, and seven times on the seventh day. Speak of the great shout that the people made when they marched around the seventh time on the seventh day, and have the walls fall, and the men all enter the city.

STORY.—A TRUE SOLDIER.

"Please come here a minute, Harvey," called his mother.

"In just a minute," came the answer. His mother waited a moment, then another, three, four, five, and still the boy did not come.

THE FALL OF JERICHO.

"Come, Harvey."

"Yes, mamma, in just a minute."

When Harvey appeared at Mrs. Curtis's side, his mother said, "Will you please go down to the store and get some butter?" but she said nothing about his delay in coming when she called.

Harvey started for the store, singing to himself, "I'm a little soldier of the heavenly King."

When he had done the errand, and again came into the room where his mother was, she held out a paper soldier's cap and belt, and asked him which he thought would make the better gun, a yard-stick or the feather duster.

"O, the feather duster would not do at all. I suppose the yard-stick will have to do, but a real gun would be so much better. Can I begin playing soldier now?"

"Yes, you may begin at once; only I want you to act just as real soldiers do. To-night I will ask papa to cut you out a gun from wood. How would that do?"

"O, that would be splendid! What do soldiers do besides march, mamma?"

"They have regular drill every day; then they have 'dress parade.' They have to learn to obey orders instantly. When the captain gives a command, it must be carried out at once. No reasons are ever asked; no waiting is allowed. Just as soon as the captain speaks, the thing must be done. Now, if you will stand, I will tell you some of the orders that are given, and show you how to carry them out. Remember that whatever the captain says must be done at once."

Then for ten minutes the room rung with "Carry arms," "Right shoulder arms," "Parade rest." Harvey enjoyed the drill very much, but after ten minutes his mother gave the order, "Break ranks, march." He was just going to say, "O, please, mamma, why can't we play a little longer?" when he remembered what his mother had said about asking no reasons; and so he kept still.

"When the drill is over," said Mrs. Curtis, "the soldiers are allowed to go where they please and to do whatever they like, if they do not disobey instructions. Each soldier knows what are the rules of the company, and has to obey them."

Day after day Harvey and his mother played soldier. He drilled once or twice a day, and liked it greatly, especially after his father made him the wooden gun. Mrs. Curtis told him many stories of the bravery and noble deeds of distinguished soldiers, and Harvey began to hope that sometime he, too, might do some great thing.

One day, however, he forgot to behave like a soldier. When his mother reminded him that he had not filled the wood-box that day, he answered: "There is wood enough to kindle the fire, and I don't see why I have to keep the box full all the time. When that is gone, I will get some more wood."

Mrs. Curtis rose, and, taking Harvey by the hand, led him to the closet and said, "This is the guard-house; I shall be obliged to place you under guard," and, leaving him in the closet, she went back to her work.

Ten minutes later she called Harvey to her, and said: "In any army the soldiers are divided into companies, over which captains are placed. Each soldier must do whatever his captain commands. Over the captains are other officers, so that each captain must obey the orders of the next higher in rank, the colonel. Over the whole army is the general. All in the army obey him. Every soldier does just as the general says, but he does not give his orders to each soldier himself. The general gives the orders to the officer under him in rank, and so on down until the captain tells the soldiers what they are to do. Now, would it do for one of the soldiers to ask, 'Why should I do this thing in this particular way?' Perhaps the captain does not know why the order has been given. You see it would not do. So it is with us. We are soldiers, as you like to sing, and Harvey is one of the soldiers in mamma's company. She is your captain. She, too, has had her directions from her higher officer, from the highest officer. Do you know whom I mean?"

Harvey went away to his work a very thoughtful boy. It was several weeks later when on coming into the room unexpectedly he heard his father say: "I think Harvey has turned over a new leaf. He minds promptly whenever he is spoken to, and never asks why."

"Yes," answered his mother, as she drew the boy to her side, "he is becoming a true soldier and a brave soldier of the heavenly King." — *Child's Hour.*

LESSON XXVIII.

RUTH.

" Thy people shall be my people, and thy God my God." — Ruth 1 : 16.

ONCE in a while comes a time when there is but little food. The barley and wheat do not grow, and so cannot be made into bread, and the people are often hungry. Such a time is called a famine. You remember there was famine in Canaan when Joseph was in Egypt and his brethren came down to buy corn. A number of years afterward there was another famine; and a man named Elimelech, with his wife Naomi and their two boys, left Canaan and went to Moab, where there was food. They lived in Moab a number of years; their sons grew older and married. The name of one of the wives was Orpah, and that of the other was Ruth.

Elimelech and Naomi with their two sons and their wives were very happy together; but Elimelech died and the two sons, and Naomi and Ruth and Orpah were left alone. Naomi was very lonely in this strange land of Moab, so far from her own home, and among people who did not love her God; for the people of Moab did not know about God. She had been happy even in this strange land, but now that the ones she loved so much were gone she felt sad. She wished to go back to her own people.

She told her daughters-in-law that she was going to Canaan, bade her friends good-by, and started for her own land. Ruth and Orpah set out with her,

RUTH.
From a painting by Brück-Lajos.

but after going a little way Naomi bade them return to their own homes. She told them that she was going to a country and to a people that they did not know, and that they had better stay with their own friends. Orpah kissed her mother-in-law and returned to her father's house, but Ruth said, "Entreat me not to leave thee, and to return from following after thee: for whither thou goest, I will go; and where thou lodgest, I will lodge: thy people shall be my people, and thy God my God." Ruth loved Naomi and wished to be with her. She loved God and longed to be with the people who knew and worshipped him. She felt that her life was better and happier since she had known the true God, and she wanted to be with his people.

Naomi and Ruth went together to Bethlehem, where Naomi had lived before she went to Moab. They were very poor, and must work to get food to eat. When they reached the town, it was harvest time. In all the fields the reapers were busy cutting the barley and storing it in barns. As Moses had commanded, it was the custom to permit the poor to go behind the reapers and pick up for themselves what was scattered. So Ruth went to the harvest field to glean behind the harvesters.

This field belonged to a man named Boaz who was a relative of Naomi. When he saw Ruth in the field, he asked one of his young men who she was; and, when he knew that she had come with Naomi, he was very kind to her and gave her dinner with his maidens and men. He also told his young men to let handfuls of the barley fall that she might glean them. When Ruth thanked him for his kindness and asked him why he was so good to her, a stranger, he said that it was because she had left her people and her gods, and had come to live with them and serve the true God.

The next day Ruth again went to the field belonging to Boaz, who was even more kind; he was pleased because she carried whatever she had to Naomi.

After a time Ruth became the wife of Boaz, and had a good home and a kind and loving husband. She was looked up to and respected by all, as her husband was one of the chief men of the place. I am sure she did not forget Naomi, but made the rest of her life as happy as possible.

Thus God blessed Ruth because she had chosen him and his people. When she had come to Canaan, among the people who loved God, she at once received kindness and help. Then she found a good home where she was tenderly loved and cared for by her husband. She was no longer lonely and sad, but her life was bright and full. Besides all this, God was her God, and he could give her peace and joy such as she could have in no other way. It was just as it is with us; if we try to do God's will, he makes us happy as we cannot be if we do not do as he wishes.

One more great blessing God gave to Ruth,—a little son whom she called Obed. His grandson was David, the sweet singer who wrote such beautiful psalms. After a long time David's descendant was the little child Jesus, God's own Son, whom he sent on earth to help and bless us all. Thus Ruth, because she chose God and his people, became the mother of a little boy whose son's son way down many generations was God's own Son Jesus. Happy Ruth to be so blessed by God!

MEMORY GEM.

Little Miss Selfish and Lend-a-Hand
Went journeying up and down the land.
On Lend-a-Hand the sunshine smiled,
The wild flowers bloomed for the happy child,

Birds greeted her from every tree;
But Selfish said, "No one loves me."

Little Miss Selfish and Lend-a-Hand
Went journeying home across the land.
Miss Selfish met with trouble and loss;
The weather was bad, the folks were cross;
Lend-a-Hand said, when the journey was o'er,
"I never had such a good time before."

— *Selected.*

OCCUPATION.

Scatter small bits of straw or tiny sticks over the table to represent the barley in the field. Have longer sticks or figures represent the men and maidens. Allow the children to rake up the straw as would the reapers, taking care to leave little handfuls here and there to be gathered up by another child who moves one of the sticks along to represent Ruth. Be sure that Ruth carries her barley to the house built at one side, which she and Naomi call home.

STORY.—MASTER DON'T-WANT-TO OR MISS LOVE-ALL.

Master All-Right and little Miss Yes-Mamma were walking hand in hand down the street, when naughty Don't-Want-To tripped them up, and they both fell flat on their faces. Up ran Miss Oh-Dear, followed by Master Boo-Hoo, and jumped on top of the others. A crowd very quickly gathers whenever anything unusual occurs on the street, and soon Miss Don't-Care and Miss I-Won't were racing to the spot, followed by Masters Stop-It and Sha'n't.

Dirty little street gamins and naughty boys and girls were not the only children to hurry to the spot, for soon Miss Love-All and Sir I'll-Try came around the corner. At sight of them Miss I-Won't hurried away with Stop-It and Sha'n't. Love-All whispered something to Don't-Care, who suddenly disappeared and in her place stood Please-Excuse-Me. Naughty Don't-Want-To, frightened at the result of what he had done, quickly slipped away. Smiling-Face and Never-Mind came up and carried away Miss Oh-Dear and Master Boo-Hoo, so that All-Right and Yes-Mamma were left with Love-All and I'll-Try.

The four walked on down the street until they came to a pretty little cottage with a tiny flower-garden and a narrow strip of grass in front, and a white fence that looked as if it had lately been painted, it was so clean and fresh. Indeed, the paint was hardly dry, for all the day before Master All-Right and Sir I'll-Try had worked in the hot sun, moving the paint-brushes up and down the pickets of that particular fence; for you must know that this is where Master All-Right lives, and Sir I'll-Try is always ready to help in any good work that Master All-Right wishes to do.

The children separated here, and Love-All and I'll-Try went down a side street, calling to the others as they went, "Let us know any time you want us." All-Right turned in at his own gate, and Yes-Mamma went on up the hill to her own stately home. Her mother met her at the door, and said, "Have you had a pleasant time, dear?"

Little Miss Yes-Mamma then told all about her afternoon's experience. When she had finished, her mother said, "I am sorry that my little daughter knows so many naughty boys and girls. Now we will go and arrange the flowers. Please find little Miss Helper. O, here she comes. Now who will pick me the pansies?" continued the mother.

Before she had finished asking the question, a

little voice close by asked, "What for?" while another voice as quickly said, "I will." When mamma asked for some water for the thirsty little flowers, naughty little Why popped up, but Good-Little-Girl ran and brought it at once.

Soon the flowers were all arranged, and mamma said that it was time to go to bed, and at once naughty Don't-Want-To, who had started all the trouble, came back. Mamma looked grieved and said, "Where is my Good-Little-Girl?"

The Good-Little-Girl did not come, however, and at last the mamma had to call Miss Mind to talk with her little daughter. Then the Good-Little-Girl came again, and when the mother asked whether she was ready to go to bed, she cheerfully answered, "Yes, mamma."

Just at this time Master All-Right came in on an errand for his mother; and, as he was not in haste, he stayed and listened to the story that the mother was ready to tell of the knights of olden time, and of how they used to go out to do battle with wicked giants and how they overcame their enemies. She told them that Don't-Want-To was an enemy, and that they both ought to have nothing to do with him. They did not need to fight with swords, but they ought to shun his company, and they would find it hard work to prevent his being with them.

"It is possible," she said, "to drive him away, so that he will never trouble you if you persist in not playing with him or having anything to do with him. The same is true of the other naughty children whose names even I dislike."

The children then bade each other good night, while All-Right ran home and Yes-Mamma went up to her room.

And now can you tell why somebody told you this story for this Sunday's lesson? — *Child's Hour.*

LESSON XXIX.

SAMUEL.

"Speak, Lord, for thy servant heareth." — *1 Sam. 3 : 9.*

THERE was a woman in Israel who felt very sad because she had no children. Her husband was kind to her, but she wanted a little son. They lived so far from the temple, their church, that they could not often go; but one time when they went she prayed to God and asked him to send her a little child. She prayed very earnestly, and she promised that, if God should send her a son, he should be given to the Lord to serve God all his life. The priest in the temple who saw her praying so earnestly blessed her and she went to her home.

She no longer was sad, for she felt that her prayer would be answered; and it was. God sent her a little son, and she called his name Samuel because, she said, she had asked him of God.

As soon as he was old enough to be away from his mother all the time she took him up to the temple, and left him with the priest Eli, who was then an old man. She was sorry to have her little son so far away from her, for she loved him dearly; but she had promised to "lend him to the Lord," and she was glad to have him do God's work.

Samuel helped Eli with all the work of the temple, and did just as the priest said. Each year his mother made clothing for him, which she carried when she came to worship at the temple. The Bible says,

"The child Samuel grew on, and was in favor both with the Lord, and also with men." It is always so when we try to do what is right; we not only make those about us love us, but we also please God.

Eli became a very old man, and Samuel took care of all the things about the temple. One night, after he had gone to bed as usual, Samuel distinctly heard some one call him. He ran to Eli, as he thought it must be that he wanted him, and said, "Here am I; for thou calledst me." The priest said, "I called not; lie down again." Samuel obeyed; but soon the same voice called again, "Samuel," and he ran back to Eli and said, "Here am I; for thou calledst me." Then Eli understood that God must have called little Samuel, so he said, "Go, lie down: and it shall be, if he call thee, that thou shalt say, Speak, Lord; for thy servant heareth."

He went back to his little bed as Eli had commanded, and soon he heard the voice as before, "Samuel, Samuel"; and then he answered as Eli told him, "Speak; for thy servant heareth."

Think of this little boy, Samuel, so far away from his father and mother, living with an old man whose heart was sad because the people of God did wrong. Now God called in the night to him, and said, "Samuel, Samuel." The little boy was not afraid, but answered, "Speak; for thy servant heareth." When you pray, you speak to God just as much as Samuel did then. It is just as solemn, and you are just as really talking to him as little Samuel was.

Then God told Samuel that he knew how wicked some of the people had become, and that he must punish them. Even the sons of Eli, the priest, did wrong things and must suffer.

In the morning Eli asked Samuel what it was that God had said to him. At first Samuel did not wish to say, because he knew it would make Eli feel sad to know how wicked his sons were and that they must be punished. But, when Eli asked him to tell all that God had said, Samuel did as Eli wished. Then Eli answered, "It is the Lord: let him do what seemeth him good." It was very hard for Eli, because he loved his sons. It always makes fathers and mothers sad when their boys or girls do wrong. But Eli knew that whatever God did was right. Do you not think that he was glad to have little Samuel with him and still more glad that Samuel tried to do just as God wished?

When Samuel grew older, he became God's prophet; that means that God often talked with him and told him what he wanted him to do and what he wished the people to do. Samuel tried to have the people do right, to do just what would please God.

Samuel was greatly blessed because he knew God, and often talked with him and tried to please him always. His mother Hannah was also very happy because God had so blessed her son, her little Samuel.

MEMORY GEM.

Now the light has gone away,
Saviour, listen while I pray,
Asking thee to watch and keep,
And to send me quiet sleep.
— *From the German.*

OCCUPATION.

Build with the blocks the temple with the courts around it. In one of these place the two pallets, one for the bed of Eli, and one for that of Samuel. Let the figure that represents Samuel go over to the other bed to answer the call, but make the point clear to the children that it was God who called.

STORY.—MARY'S DAILY BREAD.

A little girl and her mother lived alone in one room at the top of a house. You would not have cared to live there; for there were no playthings, no comfortable chairs, and no beautiful pictures about the room. The room was very bare. The little girl's mother was sick, and she could not work to earn money, and the father was far away. It was morning, and little Mary had dressed herself. Then she knelt down by the bedside, and said slowly, "Give us this day our daily bread." She knew what that meant, for the night before she had gone to bed without any supper.

After she had prayed she went into the street and began to wonder where God kept his bread. She looked up to the sky, and wondered whether he would drop it down to her. She looked at the trees in a tiny park two streets away, and wished the bread grew upon them.

Finally she turned around the corner, and saw a large, well-filled baker's shop. Mary looked into the window; and, seeing the loaves of bread, she thought to herself, "This is the place."

So she entered confidently, and said to the big baker, "I have come for it."

"Come for it? what do you mean?"

"Come for my daily bread. I'll take two, one for mother and one for me," and she pointed to the large loaves of fresh bread.

"All right," said the baker, putting them in a bag and handing them to her.

Mary started at once for the street, when he called, "Come back here; where is your money?"

"I have n't any," she said.

"Have n't any money?" he repeated; "then why do you come for the bread?"

The little girl was frightened, and burst into tears, and said: "My mother is sick and I am hungry. In my prayer I said, 'Give us this day our daily bread,' and then I thought God meant me to get it, and so I came here."

The rough but kind-hearted baker was touched by the child's simple tale, and instead of chiding her he asked her about her mother and how long she had been ill. Then, filling a large basket with bread and other food, he said, "You dear child, take this to your mother, and when you need more come to me."

LESSON XXX.

SAUL AND DAVID.

"David took the harp, and played with his hand: so Saul was refreshed, and was well, and the evil spirit departed from him."— *1 Sam. 16 : 23.*

THE children of Israel wished for a king such as the other nations about them had. They asked Samuel to give them a king. Samuel knew that it was much better for them to obey God than to have a man reign over them. God had brought them out of Egypt, had taken care of them in the wilderness, had given them food and water, and had finally brought them into the promised land.

God told Samuel to do as the people wished, but to tell them that they would not be as happy with a king as they were when God led them. God told Samuel to make Saul their king. Now Saul was very tall and fine-looking, and the people were pleased to have him for their king; but they soon found that Saul could not conquer their enemies as God had done, and that he was not so kind to them.

After a time Saul began to do wrong. He did not do what would please God. The king's servants suggested that they should find some one who could play beautifully upon the harp, and that, whenever Saul felt unhappy and wicked thoughts came to him, the player should bring his harp and play soft, sweet music to drive away the bad feelings. Saul was pleased with this plan, and told his servants to find some one who could do this.

In the little town of Bethlehem lived a lad who tended his father's sheep. He went with them to the meadows where the sweet green grass grew that the sheep loved to eat. He watched over them that no harm should come to them. He was not afraid of any wild animal, and would allow nothing to hurt his flocks. When the grass was all eaten in one place, he would lead them to another pasture where they would find plenty more. If one of the little lambs grew tired, he would tenderly take it up in his arms and carry it. When the sheep were thirsty, he led them to water. He carefully watched them to see that no one of them strayed away from the rest and was lost. This boy was the great-grandson of Ruth, the Moabitess, who chose to live with God's people; and his name was David. He loved music, and often played to himself as he wandered along the banks of the river with his sheep. He wrote beautiful poetry, and loved all the wonderful things about him that God had made. He had been taught to love his country and his own people with a deep love, but to love God most of all.

So David, while he led his sheep through sweet fields, thought much about these things. He would sing with his voice, and softly touch his harp with his fingers.

One day a messenger from Saul the king came to his father Jesse and asked him to send David that he might play the harp for King Saul.

David left his home with its beautiful pastures, its feeding flocks and quiet peacefulness, and went to the king's palace. David played the harp for Saul until it soothed and comforted him and he felt better and happier. David also was glad because he could help the king and because he was pleasing God.

Thus, whenever Saul was troubled and the evil thoughts came to him, then "David took the harp and played with his hand; so Saul was refreshed, and was well."

Do you think children have any gifts that they can use to help others feel better, or to give pleasure to those about them?

MEMORY GEM.

God make my life a little song
That comforteth the sad;
That helpeth others to be strong
And makes the singer glad.
— *M. Bentham-Edwards.*

OCCUPATION.

Make Saul's camp at one side of the table, using any rich or beautiful things to typify the abode of the king. At the other side of the table have David tending his sheep. This may be more or less elaborate as the teacher chooses. The grass may be represented, or the pool of water by which the sheep are feeding, or the sheep and shepherd alone may be used. The messenger should be sent from the king to Bethlehem and return with David. Show the children a picture of an old harp.

STORY.—THE BIRD AND THE SMILE.

Florence and May were lying together on the grass late one warm afternoon in June. The fields were full of white and gold daisies. The air was sweet with the scent of clover. The bees hummed drowsily as they flitted from blossom to blossom gathering their last loads before going to bed. The birds were beginning to sing their evening songs of thanksgiving. Both little girls were hot and tired, and lay quietly looking at the flowers' faces around them or up into the beautiful blue sky above, as they listened to the sweet songs.

At last Florence said, "I wish I had a bird of my own; then I could hear him sing all the time."

As Florence spoke, she heard the sweetest, most musical laugh, almost like the trill of a bird, and quickly looked up to see where it came from.

May also looked, and saw a little fay dressed in a robe of white that shone and sparkled in the sunlight with all the colors of the rainbow; but she hardly glanced at the dress, for the face was so much more beautiful. Although the fay was small, May saw the deep, clear eyes that looked full of love and truth, the firm, sweet mouth that she longed to hear speak again. Better than all this was the pleasant smile that made May grow glad and happy as she looked into the joyous face.

"I will give you a bird for your own, if you will always treat it well," said the fay.

"O, I will! I will! I won't forget to give it food and water, and I will be so kind to it."

"My bird needs no seed nor any drink; but you will need to help it each day, for I shall put it in your own throat. If you listen to the birds about you and try to sing as they do, the bird in your throat will learn to trill and warble as they do; but you must not get tired of practising."

"I will try not to," soberly answered Florence, for she remembered that sometimes she fretted when her mother wished her to learn a new tune.

"One more thing you must remember," continued the fay. "If you try to give pleasure with your bird, it will grow strong and learn to sing more sweetly; but, if you do not try to use it to make others happy, the bird's song will not be as beautiful and he cannot sing as loud."

May had been listening all this time and watching the fay's lovely face. Then she said, "Will you give me a bird also, that I, too, may make others happy?"

"Your lips can give pleasure if you always say kind things, but my special gift to you shall be a 'sunshine smile.' You will need to be careful of it as your sister of her bird. If you frown or look cross, the smile cannot be as bright. But, if you try to make all about you glad, then the sunshine will grow in your face."

Before the children could thank the kind fay she was gone, and they sat looking at each other. May seemed so happy and her smile was so much like sunshine that Florence began to sing a song so sweet that their mother's tired face brightened as she told the children it was time to come into the house.

There were times when Florence grew weary of the routine of practice, or did not always use the bird to make others happy; then her throat felt as if the bird had become a lump that hurt her and made her feel like crying. But, when she tried to please others, then the bird seemed to sing and warble for very joy.

The more May used the "sunshine smile," the sweeter it grew and the happier May became.

LESSON XXXI.

DAVID AND JONATHAN.

"Behold, how good and how pleasant it is for brethren to dwell together in unity!" — Ps. 133: 1.

SAUL took David to his own house to live, and David spent all his time with Saul instead of going to Bethlehem to his father's house. Saul had a son named Jonathan, and he and David were together a great deal and loved each other. They were like two brothers; only they never quarrelled. I think that Jonathan must have loved to hear David play the harp and that he was very proud of his friend. They often went to walk together and loved to talk with each other. It says in the Bible, "The soul of Jonathan was knit with the soul of David, and Jonathan loved him as his own soul."

Jonathan and David made a covenant because they loved each other so much. They promised to be kind to each other always and to try to help each other. Then Jonathan, the king's son, gave David his bow and arrows, his sword and girdle and fine clothes.

David did whatever Saul said, and tried to please him; and the Bible says he "behaved himself wisely." God was pleased with David, and the people praised him. But Saul did not like to have the people praise David. He wanted them to praise him. He did not do right, and so was not happy. He knew he was not doing what God wished, and so he felt cross toward David. When Jonathan found that his father no longer loved David, he went to David because he loved him so much; he told him how his father felt and that he was afraid that his father might do him some harm. So David stayed away, and Jonathan went to his father Saul and told him how much he loved David, how kind and good David had been, and how much he had done for them. Then Saul no longer felt angry, and David went again to Saul's house and played for him on his harp. David and Jonathan loved each other more than ever.

After a time Saul again felt angry and was no longer kind to David. He knew that David did what was right and pleased God, and that he himself did not do right and God was not pleased with him. Instead of trying to do better, he grew more angry because David did right. It is often true that, if we do wrong ourselves, we do not like to see others do right. It is because our own hearts are wicked.

Thus David again went away from Saul, and was with Samuel, the Lord's prophet, for some time. One day he was talking with Jonathan, and he asked him why Saul no longer loved him. Jonathan could not see how any one could help loving David, and he did not think his father would try to hurt David; but he said he would try to find out. He told David that he would come out into the field in three days and shoot arrows; if he called to the boy who was with him, "The arrows are on this side of you," then David would know that Saul was no longer angry; but, if he called, "The arrows are beyond you," David would know that he must go away.

Then Jonathan went to his home and talked with Saul his father, and he found that Saul did not love David and that he felt wicked enough to hurt him even. On the third day, Jonathan took his arrows, and with a boy went out into the field and began shooting. When the boy ran to find an arrow,

Jonathan called and said, "Is not the arrow beyond thee?" Then David knew that Saul was angry with him, and he went away and Jonathan went back to the city to his father's house.

MEMORY GEM.

I'm sorry he's naughty, and will not play;
But I'll love him still, for I think the way
To make him gentle and kind to me
Will be better shown if I let him see
I strive to do what I think is right;
And thus when I kneel in prayer to-night,
I will clasp my hands around my brother,
And say, "Little children, love one another."

OCCUPATION.

Illustrate simply the shooting of the arrows in the field. Explain this so that the children will understand how this showed David whether or not Saul was angry with him. Place the stick that represents David behind a stone. Let Jonathan and the lad with the arrows come from the city (which can be built or not as desired), and let one of the children make the lad walk along as another throws a straw ahead of him for the arrow. Then let the lad go back to the city while David and Jonathan walk together.

Make the friendship of David and Jonathan prominent, and let Saul's enmity be in the background as much as possible.

STORY.—SPOT, SMUT, AND SLY.

Mamma Evans was busy in the kitchen when she heard loud voices in the nursery and then a cry. Leaving her work, she slipped up-stairs to the nursery, and, seeing by the children's faces that there had been trouble, she asked no questions, but drew all three close to her and began to tell them a story of some little kittens.

"Kitty Gray had three little kittens, and Fred and May named them Spot, Smut, and Sly. Spot was all white except just one bit of black under her nose. Smut was black all over. Sly was black and white. The children thought them the cutest, prettiest little kittens that ever were. They played with them whenever they could; but, as both Fred and May went to school, there were long hours when the kittens did not see them.

"One day when the kittens were very small and had just got their eyes open, Kitty Gray told them that she must go away for a little while and leave them all alone, and that they must be sure to stay close to the box where they slept. The kittens soon tired of staying in the box, and began to play around. At first they kept close to the box, but after a little Spot was chasing Sly, and he forgot and ran too near the stairs, and down he fell, heels over head. Spot ran to Smut, crying, 'O! what shall we do?' But Kitty Gray was not far off, and she soon picked up Sly and brought him up-stairs, and began to lick his fur and gently wash him all over. She did not scold, as she felt that he had received punishment enough from his fall. Very soon Spot and Sly could run up and down stairs for themselves; but, as Smut was not strong, he was left alone much of the time, while the other kittens played outdoors in the bright, warm sunshine.

"One day Kitty Gray carried Smut down to the open door of the barn, and let him lie there where he could watch Spot and Sly playing outside. They were playing tag, chasing each other round and round, and sometimes Sly would catch Spot's tail and give it a little bite. At last he bit so hard that Spot ran into the barn and hid. Then Sly began to tease Smut, and say, 'Come out and play with me; it is lovely outdoors.' Smut started after, and then Sly would dodge out of sight. When Smut was tired of looking for Sly and started back toward the barn, Sly would bound out from behind some bush and roll Smut over and over until he was out of breath. By this time they were some little distance from the barn; and, when a sharp bark came from round the corner, Smut was so tired and frightened that he could not run to the barn, but had to climb a tree that was near by. Sly, however, left Smut to look out for himself and scampered to the barn, where he quickly hid. Poor Smut was greatly frightened and clung to the tree shaking with fear. The dog stood under the tree and barked and barked.

"At last Kitty Gray came home; and, seeing Smut up the tree trembling with fright, she made a bold rush at the dog, who, being a real coward, put his tail between his legs and ran away. Kitty Gray then ran up the tree and brought poor Smut down. After this Smut had to stay for several days in the box where the kittens slept.

"Before Smut was well enough to go down-stairs again, Kitty Gray took Sly and Spot off to one corner and talked to them. She told them how sorry she was that they could not play together pleasantly, and that they were not more kind to Smut, who was not strong enough to do as they did.

"'It is not Spot's fault,' said Sly; 'I was the one who got Smut way off by the tree, I did not think. I plagued Spot so that she ran away, and then I wanted some one to play with me, and led Smut so far away from the barn that he could not run back when the dog came.'

"'I am glad that you do not let Spot be blamed

if it is not her fault,' answered Kitty Gray; 'but I want you to remember that no kitty will like you if you are thoughtless or unkind or rough. Who likes a kitty when she does so? No kitty, no kitty, no kitty, no.'

"The next day Smut was able to go down and lie in the sun close to the barn door, and Spot and Sly tried to see which could do the funniest things to make Smut laugh. Smut then began to grow strong, and soon he could play with other kittens. Never again did Kitty Gray have to tell her kittens the verse, 'Who likes a kitty when she does so? No kitty, no kitty, no kitty, no.'"

As Mamma Evans finished telling the story, Frank said: "Mamma, I am afraid I was like Sly. I would not play fair with Helen, and I plagued baby. What would the verse be for me?"

"Who likes him when he does so? Nobody, nobody, nobody, no," answered Mamma Evans. Frank laid his head down in his mother's lap and tried not to cry, for he thought he was too big a boy to do that. Baby came toddling over the floor and put her little hand on Frank's head and said, "I love oo, I love oo, I love oo, oo."

At this Frank lifted up his head, and said, "That is much nicer than the other verse. I will try to make her and all the rest love me all the time after this."

Mamma Evans went back to her work, feeling that she should not be called up-stairs again to the children. — *Child's Hour.*

LESSON XXXII.

THE SHEPHERD PSALM.

"He shall feed his flock like a shepherd, he shall gather the lambs in his arm, and carry them in his bosom." — Isa. 40 : 11.

WE have talked about the boy David who played so sweetly upon the harp for King Saul, and about his love for Jonathan, the king's son. To-day we wish to learn something of the beautiful songs he sung. When David was older, he wrote many songs that we call psalms, and the people of Israel used to sing them.

Do you remember that, when Saul's messenger went to Bethlehem to ask David to go to the king's home and play for him, David was away with the sheep, caring for them? When he was a boy, David spent much of his time taking care of the flocks. Day after day he watched over them that no harm should come to them. He knew and cared for each particular one, and his sheep all knew and loved him. They would follow wherever he led them. He was a good shepherd, and he had spent many happy hours with his sheep. He knew so much about the sheep and their life that when he came to write songs for the people, when he wanted to praise God, was it any wonder that he thought of the sheep and their shepherd?

When he had been a shepherd boy, he had taken good care of the sheep, and he knew what it meant to tend the sheep carefully. Now he wanted to thank God for watching over his life; so he said,

THE GOOD SHEPHERD.
From a painting by B. Plockhorst.

"The Lord is my shepherd; I shall not want." David led the sheep to the land that was covered with sweet, green grass, and the sheep could eat or lie down and rest as they chose. He led them to the stream that they might drink the clear, cool, running water. Thus David sung of his shepherd, the Lord, "He maketh me to lie down in green pastures; he leadeth me beside the still waters." He said this because God had given him just what was best for him, as the shepherd does for his sheep.

Then David said, "He restoreth my soul." He meant that, when he felt sad, God had made him feel glad again. God showed him how to do what was right. If you were out for a walk, and did not know which path to take, and some one showed you which way to go, how glad you would be! We want to go in the path toward God, the right path. David called it the path of righteousness, and he said, "He guideth me in the paths of righteousness for his name's sake."

When the shepherd is leading his sheep to pasture, they sometimes come to a bad place, where it is rough and there are briers that hurt the sheep. Then the shepherd takes the best of care of his sheep; he holds the long crook that he carries in his hand so that it will hold back the prickly bushes and the sheep can go by without being hurt. The shepherd talks to his sheep so that they will not be afraid. Thus David said, "Yea, though I walk through the valley of the shadow of death, I will fear no evil; for thou art with me: thy rod and thy staff they comfort me." Even when he had hard things to do, God helped him just as the shepherd helps the sheep with his staff by holding back the briers.

When people come to visit us, we try to give them the best things to eat that we can; we try to do whatever is possible to please them. David said,

"Thou preparest a table before me in the presence of mine enemies: thou hast anointed my head with oil"; this was one way in which the people showed that they cared for one another. "My cup runneth over." It was as if God had made his life so happy that it was like a cup filled so full that it ran over. God had blessed him so much that he said, "Surely goodness and mercy shall follow me all the days of my life: and I will dwell in the house of the Lord forever." Could we have a better place to live than with God in his house? Thus David sung of God, his shepherd.

He is also our shepherd, and we all are like sheep whom he cares for most tenderly all the time. He fills our cups of joy full to overflowing; he leads us in good paths through a beautiful country; and, best of all, he never leaves us, but is always close by, watching over us that no harm shall come to us. We cannot see him, but he sees us and knows whatever we do. He is our loving shepherd.

MEMORY GEM.

We read in the wonderful story,
   So sweetly and tenderly told,
How Jesus the Shepherd came seeking
   The lambs that were lost from his fold.
And we who would share in his glory
   Must follow his footsteps below;
Must comfort the poor and the needy,
   The little bare feet in the snow.

OCCUPATION.

There is a card upon which is printed the Shepherd Psalm and pictures of the green pastures and flowing brook. This card is so arranged that it can be cut into ten pieces, which the children put together to make the complete card.

STORY.—THE LOST SHEEP.

There were ninety and nine that safely lay
   In the shelter of the fold,
But one was out on the hills away,
   Far off from the gates of gold —
Away on the mountains wild and bare,
Away from the tender Shepherd's care.

"Lord, thou hast here thy ninety and nine:
   Are they not enough for thee?"
But the Shepherd made answer: "This of mine
   Has wandered away from me,
And, although the road be rough and steep,
I go to the desert to find my sheep."

But none of the ransomed ever knew
   How deep were the waters crossed;
Nor how dark was the night that the Lord passed
   through,
   Ere he found his sheep that was lost.
Out in the desert he heard its cry —
Sick and helpless, and ready to die.

"Lord, whence are those blood-drops all the way
   That mark out the mountain's track?"
"They were shed for one who had gone astray
   Ere the Shepherd could bring him back."
"Lord, whence are thy hands so rent and torn?"
"They are pierced to-night by many a thorn."

But all through the mountains, thunder-riven,
   And up from the rocky steep,
There rose a cry to the gate of heaven,
   "Rejoice! I have found my sheep!"
And the angels echoed around the throne,
"Rejoice, for the Lord brings back his own!"
                    — *E. C. Clephane.*

LESSON XXXIII.

SOLOMON'S TEMPLE.

"I purpose to build an house for the name of the Lord my God."
— *1 Kings 5 : 5.*

KING SAUL did not do what was right. He was not a good king. The people had wanted a man for their king, but they were not happy with him. God then gave them another. He made David, the sweet singer, king in place of Saul. David did many good things for his people, and tried to please God. He wished to build a house for God, and spent much time in getting beautiful and rich things together for the temple. Ever since the time of Samuel the people had been giving gold and precious things to help make a beautiful temple for God. David could not build it, however, for God had other work for him to do.

After David's death his son Solomon became king, and he went to work to have the temple built at once. He wished to have the finest wood for the temple, and he wished to have the wood cut in the very best way. He send word to Hiram, the king of Tyre, who had loved his father David and would help him, and Solomon asked him to have his men cut some of the beautiful cedar-trees which grew in his country, for the workmen of Tyre knew how.

Great blocks of white limestone were taken out of the quarries and cut into the right shapes to build the foundation. Solomon had a great army of workmen to build the temple, yet it was seven years before it was finished. It was to be the most splendid building in the world. Everything was made ready before being taken to the place where the temple was to be built. Then it could all be put together very quietly, and no noise of either hammer or axe was heard where the temple was to stand. It was all built in sacred silence.

The temple was on a mount. It was a beautiful spot upon which to have the house of God. The top of the mount was smoothed off to make a place for the great temple, and it stood so high as to be seen by all.

Let us think of the great white stones, all cut and shaped beforehand, as they are silently swung into place to build the strong foundation. Stone upon stone the building rises, till high above the city it stands, a beautiful temple of snow-white stone and glittering gold that sparkles and shines in the bright sunlight.

The inside of the magnificent temple was made of beautiful cedar-wood, or red sandalwood, and then covered with gold. This was not a thin wash of gold, but thick plates of gold fastened on with gold nails. The walls and doors were carved to look like palms, cherubim, and flowers, and then covered with gold.

The very best of everything the people had or could get from other places was used in the temple. Every part was made perfect and beautiful, whether it would show or not, because it was God's house. The people not only gave their best things, but even gave what they would have liked to keep for themselves. Nothing was too good to give for God's temple.

The temple was built, as was the tabernacle in the wilderness, with a holy place and the holy of holies. The beautiful vessels of gold and silver were placed inside, and in the holy of holies was the same ark, with the tables of stone upon which were written the ten commandments, that was in the tabernacle. Not only was the temple as beautiful and fine as it could be made, but also everything that was placed inside was of the best. Do you not think that we ought to give our best to God? Do you not think that our churches, the places we build for God's house, should be as perfect and beautiful, clean and holy, as possible?

The Bible says, "Know ye not that ye are a temple of God, and that the Spirit of God dwelleth in you?" That means that God is in our hearts, he lives with us, and we ought to make ourselves as good and pure as possible. We are like the temple where God lives; and our lips are to say only good and pure words, our hands are to do only kind and loving deeds, our minds to think only pure and holy thoughts, our hearts to love only good things. If we make our temples, that is, ourselves, as sweet and good and pure as possible, then God will love to stay with us and help us. Let us work hard to make ourselves fit to be his temples.

MEMORY GEM.

Help us, Lord, to love thee more
    Than we ever loved before;
In our work and in our play
    Be thou with us through the day.

OCCUPATION.

Let the children build the temple. Illustrate the silent placing of the great blocks of stone, the covering with gold of the interior, etc. Then have ready slips of paper the size of the blocks used to build the temple, upon which shall be written the names of the qualities which will help us to make ourselves fit temples for God to dwell in. Draw from the children, as far as possible, their idea of what will make the character good and beautiful as God desires. Write these upon the slips of paper, — unselfishness, obedience, love, reverence, etc.; place the slips upon the blocks that are the foundation of the temple.

STORY. — JOE'S LILY.

Joe had been saving his pennies since Christmas time. The boys in Miss Davis's Sunday-school class wanted to buy flowers for the church for Easter. This was not grand and beautiful as were some of the churches, but was plain and bare. The boys thought that, if they had some flowers, the room would look better. Each boy wished to buy the best flowers he could, but they were poor and had few pennies. Most of the boys earned all the money they had, and many of them helped pay for the poor rooms they called home. Some sold newspapers; Joe earned his money by blacking boots.

Three weeks before Easter, Joe counted his money and went to the florist's to see what flowers could be bought for the sum he had saved. He had set his heart upon having one of the beautiful Easter lilies, but he found that he had not nearly enough to buy so costly a flower. The next day he did not buy himself a dinner, but had only a glass of milk. The place where he had his blacking-box was so far away that he could not go to his own home for dinner. Each day he took only the glass of milk at noon. The day before Easter he found that he had just enough money to buy the coveted lily.

The other boys had also worked hard for their flowers. One had bought hyacinths, another some white pinks, while one of the boys had some callas. Miss Davis had once told the boys that white meant pure and clean, and they felt that nothing but white flowers was good enough.

Easter Sunday was a beautiful day, and Joe and the other boys were up very early. They had many things to do before they could go to the church. They wanted to carry their flowers early, so that Miss Davis might have time to arrange them prettily. They were so early that even Miss Davis had not come. As she came into the door and saw the beautiful white flowers, a sunny smile came to her face that made the boys very happy. She knew they had been trying to buy some flowers, but had not thought that they would be able to get so many or so lovely ones. She knew that the boys were poor and that they must have given up many things to buy the flowers. She was so pleased she hardly knew what to say to them; but it made no difference, for they knew from her face that she was glad.

"Do you think they are good enough, Miss Davis?" asked Joe.

"Yes indeed! They are beautiful; nothing could be sweeter to bring to God's house. The flowers that God made cannot be better used than to make his house fragrant."

"I wanted to buy white roses," said Tom, "but they cost too much." And he looked fondly at the hyacinths he had brought.

"These are just as good," answered Miss Davis, "and I am sure that God will be pleased because you have tried so hard to get the best for him. When we give up our own things for him, we are like Jesus. These hyacinths are as pure and lovely as any roses could be, and much sweeter."

"I bought my lily early yesterday morning, Miss Davis, so I could take it home for Nell to look at through the day. I was afraid it might wither, but I did want her to have a little bit of it," continued Joe.

"After the service is all over, I hope you boys will take the flowers to some of your friends."

"Can we take some to Pete? You know he has been sick most a month," said Tom.

"That would be a good plan. It always seems to me as though the flowers should go to those who have to lie still in bed. I wonder why you all brought white flowers," asked Miss Davis.

"O, because you said they were so pure and clean, and we see so much that is dirty that we wanted the cleanest thing we could find."

"Do you know that these flowers can be a part of you, boys? Do you know that you can be like these white lilies? When you look at the flower, can you think of its saying anything wrong? If you let no naughty words come from your lips, they will be like the petals of the flower pure and clean. The flower brings joy and pleasure to those about it. You can do kind little acts which will please others. Even the stem of the flower, looking so smooth and green, makes one think of the woods and running brooks and dancing sunlight. If your faces always carry a smile, people will be glad to see you come into the room. Just one thing more. Look down into the heart of this lily. See the golden little stamens. Your hearts can be golden if you think only good thoughts."

LESSON XXXIV.

SOLOMON'S PROVERBS.

" A good name is rather to be chosen than great riches." — Prov. 22 : 1.

A SHORT time after Solomon became king, before he had built the great temple, he went to Gibeon to pray to God and to worship him. In the night God appeared to him in a vision, and said, "Ask what I shall give thee." What would Solomon ask? Would it be that he might be king a long time, that he might be very rich, that he might always be happy, that his enemies should not fight against him, or that he should be loved by all the people? Solomon did not ask for any of these things.

He prayed that God would give him wisdom that he might know how to do right in all things; that he might know what to do for the great nation, the children of Israel, over whom he was the king. Solomon's choice pleased God greatly. It was the best thing he could have asked for, to know how to do what was right in God's eyes. Then the Lord promised to grant his wish, and said that he should also have riches and honor, and a long life besides, and that God would make him more famous than any king that had ever lived.

God did as he promised, and made Solomon very wise. He is said to have been the wisest man who ever lived, and because he was so wise he wrote many things to teach the people. These sayings are called proverbs, and are just as much of a help to you and me now as they were to the children of

Israel, for whom they were written. Solomon tells the children that they should not forget God's laws and that they should keep his commandments.

One of his proverbs I wish to tell you about to-day. Let us think carefully and see whether we can understand it. "A good name is rather to be chosen than great riches." To have a "good name" means to be thought well of by others, to be liked by them, to be kind and unselfish and loving so that those about us shall be glad when we are with them. Solomon says that this is rather to be chosen than great riches, that it is better than to have lots of money.

Now money is a good thing to have if it is rightly used. We need it to buy clothes and food, to pay for houses that shall protect us from the rain and snow, to help others, and to send people to the children who do not know about Jesus and to tell them of his love. But some people think more about getting money than about anything else; some people think more of their beautiful homes than of what is right; some people care more to do what other people do than to please God; and they are all wrong.

God knows everything that we do, whether any one else sees or not; he knows all our thoughts; he knows whether we feel kind and loving to those about us, or whether we have naughty thoughts in our hearts. If we really have a "good name," we shall please God. He will know whether we are doing the best we can at all times, whether or not we do what is right when no one sees us.

We may do something when mamma or teacher is out of the room and we think that no one sees, but God knows and we have not a "good name." We may think naughty thoughts, or feel ugly and selfish as if we would like to do something wrong; yet, if we do not do the wrong thing, mamma may not know of the bad thoughts, but God does. Let us try to live so that God shall look into our hearts, into our thoughts, and see that all is right; then he will give us a "good name."

MEMORY GEM.

Beautiful eyes are those that show,
Like crystal panes where the hearth-fires glow,
Beautiful thoughts that burn below.

OCCUPATION.

Have drawn on one side of the blackboard a child's face, one that is sweet and good. On the other side of the board have a drawing of the same face with an ugly frown that shows the naughty temper within. The child may not appear to be naughty as mamma looks at him; but, if she could look into his heart as God can, she would see the picture upon the other side of the board.

STORY.—THOUGHT ECHOES.

A long time ago, when this earth was first made, there were a great many Echo Elves. They loved the rocky hills and the quiet lakes; they clung to every crevice and point of rock. They were always listening and watching for sounds; and, when they heard one, they repeated it again and again. Sometimes they trilled the last notes of a bird's song; sometimes they answered the monkey's chatter; and sometimes they thundered as the ocean beat against the rocks.

Then there were elves who caught up the thoughts that were floating around. When the squirrel, frisking about, found a sweet nut and lifted his head in thankfulness to God, the Thought Echoes repeated again and again the thanks of the squirrel. When the flowers lifted their faces to the welcome dew and smiled in their gladness, then the Thought Elves echoed the happy song till all around joined in it. The Echo Elves never tired of their play. They loved to repeat the sweet sounds they heard, or the lovely thoughts.

After a long time people came upon the earth, and the Echo Elves were happier than ever. They grew more fond of music and they would listen for the children's laughter. One day a little child wandered down by a pond dotted with white lilies, and exclaimed, " O, see the beautiful stars ! "

And the Echo Elves answered, " Beautiful stars."

"They 've come down from the sky," said the child.

" From the sky," said the Echoes.

" They 've come to play with me," said the child.

" Play with me," answered the Echoes.

" I love them ! I love them ! " said the child.

" Love them ! Love them ! " said the Elves.
And they also loved the child, for they loved all that was good and true.

Many of the Echo Elves were very happy after the coming of people upon the earth, but the Thought Echoes had a hard time. They loved the good and beautiful thoughts, but the bad thoughts hurt them. Whenever a child felt cross in his heart, the Thought Echoes had to repeat the thought even though it made them sad. They could not echo it as loud as when all had been happy thoughts. Then other people had bad thoughts, and the Echoes grew so weak that they could only whisper. After this no person could hear the Thought Echoes.

All this was long, long ago, but the Echoes still live on the earth ; they still love to answer the laughter and song of the children ; they are still very fond of music. I am sure many of you have heard them. The Thought Echoes are here also; they know what each one is thinking, and they whisper their thoughts. You and I cannot hear them, but there is One who hears and understands each Thought Echo.

As the little child looked at the beautiful pond-lilies he thought to himself, "They are so white and clean."

"White and clean," whispered the Thought Echoes.

"I want to be like them," thought the child.

"Like them," whispered the Echoes.

The Thought Echoes would have been glad to shout the words for all to hear, but they could not. Still they knew there was One who could hear, and they were glad the thoughts were sweet and good as he would listen to them.

If only all the thoughts were loving and gentle, how glad the Thought Echoes would be! Then they could answer as do the other Echo Elves. Even more glad would be the One who hears every thought that the Thought Echoes repeat. It makes him very happy when our thoughts are right and beautiful.

THE PITCHER OF TEARS.
From a painting by Paul Thumann.

LESSON XXXV.

ELIJAH.

"The barrel of meal shall not waste, neither shall the cruse of oil fail." — *1 Kings* 17 : 14.

I WONDER whether we all remember the story of little Samuel. He lived in the temple with the priest Eli, and one night God called to him. Afterward, when he grew to be a man, he was one of God's prophets. To-day we are to learn of another of the "men of God." This man's name was Elijah, and he tried to do just as God wished, but the people about him were very wicked. God's own chosen people did wrong.

You remember that God talked with his prophets and told them what to do. God told Elijah that there was to be a famine in Canaan and there would not be enough food. God told Elijah to go to a brook called Cherith where he would give him food to eat. Elijah did as God said. He had plenty of water to drink at the brook; but nothing grew there, and what should Elijah eat? But God had promised to care for him, and Elijah believed God.

In the morning some ravens brought him bread and meat. At night the ravens again came with meat and bread. Day after day the birds brought food to the prophet, until at last the water in the brook was all dried up because there had been no rain.

Then God told Elijah to go to a place called Zarephath and live with a widow whose home was there. As the prophet was on his way toward her house, he saw this very woman gathering small sticks with which to make a fire. You see she must have been poor. Elijah asked her to bring him a little water to drink, for he was very thirsty after his long walk. She gladly brought the water, for she had plenty. Then the prophet asked her to bring him some bread, for he was hungry.

The poor woman felt very sad. She would have been glad to give him food, but how could she? She said that she had not a bit of bread or cake or food of any kind in the house; she had only a little bit of meal in a barrel, and a little oil which she used in mixing the meal. She told the prophet that she was gathering wood with which to make a fire to cook that last bit of meal for herself and her son, and that then they would have nothing left.

Elijah told her not to be troubled about it, but to go and make the cake and bring him some; and he said to her, "Thus saith the Lord, the God of Israel, The barrel of meal shall not waste, neither shall the cruse of oil fail, until the day that the Lord sendeth rain upon the earth."

The widow believed what the prophet told her, and quickly went and made the cake and brought it to him. Then Elijah lived with her, and what he had promised proved true. Each day, when she made the cake for them all to eat, there was as much meal left in the barrel after she had taken all she needed for their food for the day as before she took it out; so they had plenty to eat.

I cannot tell you how it happened that there was as much meal left in the barrel as if she had not taken any out, except that God made it so. He was taking care of his prophet Elijah, and because the woman was willing to share the last food she had with Elijah God took care of her and her son also.

Does God care for us now and give us food? Who sends the warm sunshine to make the wheat and corn grow? Who makes the rain come pattering down that the plants shall have water to drink and not be thirsty? Could the wheat and the corn grow and ripen without the sunshine and rain? Could we make bread or corn-cake without wheat and corn? What should we do if the brooks and springs all dried up so that there was no water for us to drink? Who made the gentle, brown-eyed cows that give us such sweet, good milk?

We see that God gives us food and drink now just as much as he did when Elijah lived upon the earth so many, many years ago. He takes just as loving care of us now as he did then, and he is just as much pleased when we do right, or as much grieved if we do what is wrong.

MEMORY GEM.

The tall trees in the greenwood,
  The pleasant summer sun,
The ripe fruits in the garden,
  He made them every one.

OCCUPATION.

Let the figure to represent Elijah sit by a brook that may be represented by a strip of paper, and let paper ravens fly down to him. It seems best not to try to illustrate the renewal of the widow's meal and oil, since we have not the miraculous power of refilling the barrel and cruse.

STORY.—THE OPEN DOOR.

Poor Mrs. Van Loon was a widow. She had four children. The eldest was Dirk, a boy of eight years.

One evening she had no bread, and her children were hungry. She folded her hands, and prayed to God; for she served the Lord, and she believed that he loved and could help her.

When she had finished her prayer, Dirk said to her, "Mother, don't we read in the Bible that God sent ravens to a pious man to bring him bread?"

"Yes," answered the mother. "But that was long, long ago, my dear."

"Well," said Dirk, "then the Lord may send ravens now. I'll go and open the door, else they can't fly in."

In a trice Dirk jumped to the door, which he left wide open, so that the light of the lamp fell on the pavement of the street.

Shortly after, the burgomaster passed by. The burgomaster is the first magistrate of a Dutch town or village. Seeing the open door, he stopped.

Looking into the room, he was pleased with its clean, tidy appearance, and with the nice little children who were grouped around their mother. He could not help stepping in, and, approaching Mrs. Van Loon, he said, "Eh, my good woman, why is your door open so late as this?"

Mrs. Van Loon was a little confused when she saw such a well-dressed gentleman in her poor room. She quickly rose and dropped a courtesy to the gentleman; then, taking Dirk's cap from his head and smoothing his hair, she answered with a smile, "My little Dirk has done it, sir, that the ravens may fly in to bring us bread."

Now, the burgomaster was dressed in a black coat and black trousers, and he wore a black hat. He was quite black all over, except his collar and shirt-front.

"Ah, indeed!" he exclaimed cheerfully. "Dirk is right. Here is a raven, you see, and a large one, too. Come along, Dirk, and I'll show you where the bread is."

The burgomaster took Dirk to his house, and ordered his servant to put two loaves and a small pot of butter into a basket. This he gave to Dirk, who carried it home as quickly as he could. When the other little children saw the bread, they began dancing and clapping their hands. The mother gave to each of them a thick slice of bread and butter, which they ate with the greatest relish.

When they had finished their meal, Dirk went to the open door, and, taking his cap from his head, looked up to the sky, and said, "Many thanks, good Lord!" And after having said this he shut the door. — *John de Liefde.*

LESSON XXXVI.

THE LITTLE MAID.

"I will not forget thy word." — Ps. 119: 16.

The Bible tells us many beautiful stories of things that happened long, long ago. To-day I should like to tell you one of these. It is about a little girl; the Bible calls her a little maid, but does not tell us her name. She was one of the children of Israel, and she was a good and obedient child, who tried hard to help her mother. Her mother loved her greatly, and often talked with her. She told her little daughter about God and how much he had done for them, how he loved them and wished them to do what was right; she taught her to pray always to him and to remember that he wished her to grow up to be a loving, kind, and helpful woman.

By and by a dreadful thing happened to this little maid. She was taken away from her mother and father, from brothers and sisters, and carried off a long way to a land called Syria. She knew no one in this new place, and she was very lonely and homesick. She must have often wished that she could see her mother, even if for but a moment.

She lived with a man named Naaman, who was a great man in Syria. He had helped the king, and so was thought much of by him. But Naaman did not know about God or love him, neither did the other people in Syria. He was not a happy man; for he had a dreadful sickness, and no one had been able to cure him.

The little maiden felt very sorry for her master Naaman, and tried to please him. She was loving and kind, just as her mother had taught her to be. She waited on his wife and always tried to do the very best that she could. She wished that Naaman might be made well. Although she was so far from her own people, she had not forgotten about God or about the many wonderful things he had done for his people. She knew that in her own land there was a prophet, one of God's men called Elisha, and that God often helped him to do wonderful things.

The little maid told Naaman's wife about this prophet Elisha, who,' she thought, could cure her master Naaman of his sickness. She was so sure that he could do it that Naaman began to hope a little. He had tried many different things, and none of them had done any good. But it was a dreadful disease, and he so much wanted to be cured that he could not help trying this man of whom the little maid spoke.

Naaman went to the house of the prophet Elisha in Samaria. He rode up to Elisha's house in his chariot drawn by fine, strong horses, and sent a messenger to the door. The prophet sent him word to go to the river Jordan and bathe in the water seven times.

Do you suppose that Naaman was sick because he had not washed? Do you think that washing in the river Jordan seven times would make him well? No, neither of these two things was true; but, if Naaman obeyed the prophet and bathed in the river seven times, God would make him well.

After a time Naaman did as the prophet said, and went to the river Jordan and dipped himself in the water seven times; and he was at once perfectly well. Naaman was so happy that he went back to the house of Elisha to thank him. He was also so grateful to God that he said he would always serve him and try to please him, and that he would teach all in his house to do the same. He then knew that God had all power and could do anything, and that he loved his children.

When he returned to his own home, he was met by all the people, and great was the rejoicing that he was well again. How pleased and happy his wife must have been to see him well and strong once more!

We must not forget the little maid who had helped Naaman so much. She was very, very happy, for she knew that Naaman was well because she had told him about her God and his prophet, Elisha. She was happy because now Naaman loved and worshipped the true God. She was happy because she had done what was right, and had not forgotten what her mother had taught her, even when she was a long way off from mother, home, friends, and the people who knew and loved God.

MEMORY GEM.

Look for goodness, look for gladness;
  You will meet them all the while;
If you bring a smiling visage
  To the glass, you meet a smile.

OCCUPATION.

Build Naaman's house in Syria, and speak of the maid's message to Naaman. Have Elisha's house built in Samaria, and represent the river Jordan by string or a narrow slip of paper. Let Naaman travel from his home to that of Elisha and then to the river

Jordan, in which he bathes seven times and then returns to his home.

STORY.— A JAPANESE STORY.

A long, long time ago, there dwelt a father and mother whose little daughter was as beautiful as the sunlight itself.

But one day the father was called to the city where the king dwelt, and so was forced to say good-by to his beautiful daughter for the first time in her short life.

Now the child's mother had never been away from her home in all her life; and so, when the father went so far away, she was frightened. She was sure some dreadful thing would happen to him; and still she was very proud, for he was the first man from that town that had ever been called by the king to the great city.

At last the time came for the father to come back. The fond mother — as mothers in all time have done — dressed herself and the beautiful child in their very prettiest dresses, and together they waited his coming.

By and by he came; and he brought with him many presents for both mother and child, and besides he had marvellous stories to tell of the wonderful far-off city.

"I have brought you a most strange present," said he to his wife. "It is called a mirror, something we have never had in our village, and I think no one of us ever even heard of one before."

Then he gave the little box to his wife, saying, "Tell me what you see."

She opened it. There lay a piece of shining metal. It was ornamented with frosted silver carved in birds and flowers.

"How beautiful!" said the wife. . "How it shines! and how beautiful the birds and flowers are!"

"Look closely into it," said the husband, "and tell me what else you see."

The good wife raised it and looked into it.

"Why," she cried, "I see a beautiful woman's face. How her eyes shine! and what a bright, shining face she has! And her lips are moving as if she were talking. And — how strange! — she has a dress of blue exactly like my own!"

How the husband laughed! How proud he was that he knew something no one else in the village knew!

"Dear wife," said he, "it is your own beautiful face you see; it is your own laughing eyes; for this is a mirror, and it shows everything that is held before it."

"How wonderful!" was all the amazed wife could say; and all day long she and her little daughter looked into the mirror and laughed and talked with it.

But then it came into the thought of the mother, "How vain I am! I am very foolish."

And she hid the mirror away and never allowed herself even to take one tiny peep into it.

Years passed away; the little child had grown to be a young woman as beautiful as her own mother. Indeed, she was so exactly like her mother that one could scarcely tell them apart except that one was a little older than the other.

But one day the good mother grew very ill. She knew that she had only a few hours to live, and her heart was very heavy to think that her dear child would so soon forget her.

So she took the little mirror out from its hiding-place, and called the daughter to her.

"Dear child," said she, "I am going away to leave

you. But here is a little mirror. Promise me that every morning and night you will look into it, for you will see me there, and then you will know that I am watching over you always. When you are happy, you will see that I am happy; and, when you are sad, you will see that I am sad with you."

Then the mother died, and the child was left alone with her father.

But she was not sad, for she had the wonderful mirror. Every night and morning she looked into it and saw her mother's face looking up into hers. Every night she told the face in the mirror all that had happened during the day; and the mother spoke back always, though the daughter could not hear what she said. Whenever she had joyous news to tell, the mother's face was always joyous; and, when she had sad news to tell, the mother's face was always filled with sad sympathy.

So the child lived on, growing sweeter and lovelier every day; for she thought always only such thoughts as she would like to have her mother see, and did only those things that her mother would like to know she had done.

"Dear mother's face grows kinder and sweeter every day," said she to her father one day.

The father's eyes filled with tears, "Yes, dear child," said he, "it does; and your own face grows every day more like your mother's. And it will be so always so long as you are good and true."

One day a handsome young prince came riding through the town. "Who is that lovely maiden?" said he, as he passed the home of this sweet young woman. "For never in my life have I seen a face so sweet. Would that she might dwell with me in my palace and be my princess!"

And so it came that one day the beautiful daughter left her father's home to be a princess. And never till she reached the great city where the grand ladies all had mirrors did she know that it was her own face she had been looking into all those years.

But now she understood; and she loved her sweet mother all the more now that she knew her mother had taken this way to help her grow good and true, when she could no longer herself guide and teach her. — *From " Primary Education."*

LESSON XXXVII.

DANIEL.

"Daniel purposed in his heart that he would not defile himself." — Dan. 1 : 8.

Do you remember that, when the children of Israel were wandering through the wilderness, God told them that, if they would obey him and do just what he said, he would always care for them? Many, many times the people forgot God; they did not obey him and he was obliged to punish them. They finally did so much that was wrong that God let the king of Babylon capture the children of Israel and carry them off to his country to work for him. God felt sorry for his people, just as your father and mother feel sorry when you have done wrong and must be punished, but God knew that his children must suffer if they did wrong.

One day the king of Babylon, whose name was Nebuchadnezzar, told one of his servants to choose a number of boys from among the princes of the land and also from among the children of Israel, who were all well shaped and handsome, and were quick to learn, and had been taught so that they already knew more than most of the people. The king told one of his wise officers to teach them all that he knew himself, that these youths might become the wisest of men. Besides this the king directed that the boys should have the best of food so as to grow strong and large. The king said that they should even have food from his own table.

Among the boys chosen were four Israelites

with strange names. They were Daniel, Hananiah, Mishael, and Azariah. The prince who had the care of the youths gave them new names which were more strange than the ones they had before. He called them Belteshazzar, Shadrach, Meshach, and Abed-nego. You need not try to learn all these strange names, but when you are older you will hear them again, for the Bible tells us more about them. We will try to remember Daniel, for he did much good and pleased God, obeying him even when it was hard to do so.

God told his people not to eat certain kinds of food, and Daniel wished to do just what God said. Wine or any kind of liquor was not good for him. It would poison his blood and make him grow weak. He would not be as large and strong; he could not learn as much; and he would never be as noble and brave and great a man as if he never touched liquor. When the rich food, the meats and wines, were brought to them, Daniel told the officer that God did not wish them to eat that food or drink wine. He asked whether he and his boy friends might not have water to drink and vegetables to eat instead of the rich food and the poison wine. The officer was afraid that the boys would grow poor and ill-looking; but Daniel said, Try us for ten days, and give us just water and vegetables, and then see whether we are not as strong and well-looking as the youths who eat of the king's food. Then the officer did as Daniel asked, and at the end of ten days they were fatter in flesh and fairer in the face than any of the other boys.

The officer therefore no longer offered the king's food to these four boys, but gave them water and vegetables. Daniel thanked God that the officer was willing to give food that was good for them and would do them no harm. God blessed the four Israelitish youths, and gave them knowledge and skill in all learning and wisdom. At the end of the time that had been appointed the youths were all taken before the king, and he talked with them, and found that Daniel and Hananiah, Mishael and Azariah, were stronger and wiser than any of the other youths or any of the wise men of his kingdom. Then the king Nebuchadnezzar had these four youths with him all the time, because among all the people there were none who were as learned and wise.

Many years after Daniel lived a good man said, "Know ye not that ye are a temple of God?" If Daniel had thought of this, he would have had another reason for not touching the liquor. If we are God's temples, if our bodies are for him to live in, we should take great care to keep them clean and pure. We should not be careless and do anything that will harm our bodies. We should keep them as perfect and well as possible. We should never allow anything to make them soiled. When men smoke, they make God's temple dirty and stained. If they drink poison of any kind, they injure this wonderful temple that God has given us to keep pure for him. Some persons do not seem to understand this. Let us remember and not do anything to our bodies that will soil them or unfit them to be God's temples.

MEMORY GEM.

As some rare perfume in a vase of clay
　Pervades it with a fragrance not its own,
So, when thou dwellest in a mortal soul,
　All heaven's own sweetness seems around it thrown.

OCCUPATION.

Build the king's palace, and let the young men appear before the king in state.

STORY.—NAT'S DECISION.

It was the day before Christmas, and Nat Sprague came rushing into the house, calling, "Mother, mother, where are you?"

Then he remembered that his mother had asked him that morning to come to her wherever she was instead of calling her. Thinking of his mother and her morning talk reminded him of his muddy shoes; so he stepped back on the piazza, and carefully wiped them on the mat, and then went in through the sitting-room into the kitchen. Here he found his mother just looking into the oven, and a most delicious odor of roast turkey met him as he came into the room.

"Why, mother, what are you cooking the turkey to-day for?"

"I am cooking this for Mrs. Hammond. I greatly fear there will be little Christmas joy at her house to-morrow. I shall pack a basket with the turkey and other good things, and I thought you and I would go down with it this afternoon."

"I was going to ask you if I could go over to Charlie Howe's, but of course I will go with you if you would like to have me."

While they had been talking, Mrs. Sprague had put into a small basket a tumbler of jelly, another of cranberry sauce, a loaf of bread, a dish of butter, and some crisp stalks of celery. Then she carefully placed the turkey on a platter in another basket, and covered it over.

"Will you please lock up the house, Nat, while I put on my hat and cloak?" said Mrs. Sprague, as she went briskly out of the room and up-stairs.

The house was on the outskirts of the town, and was not large. There were three rooms on the lower floor and three above. The furniture was plain and not very new, but everything about the house seemed well cared for, and there was an air of comfort and cheer that made one feel sure it was a pleasant home and a happy household.

Soon the mother and son were walking down the street, each carrying a basket. They made several turns, and at last Mrs. Sprague said, "This is the place," and together they went up the stairs of a large building near the centre of the town.

"What a dark, gloomy stairway!" exclaimed Nat; and, as they started up another flight, he said, "I am glad I do not live here." Before they were ready to go home Nat thought again and again, "I am glad I do not live here."

Mrs. Hammond was not at home, but a boy somewhat younger than Nat told them that she would be back before long, and that she was out washing for a lady. Mrs. Sprague began to put the food she had brought into the closet, while Nat talked with the boy, whose name he found was Will.

There were two rooms, neither of which had a carpet. In one of them was an old cook-stove, a table, three wooden chairs, and a rocking-chair with one rocker broken. In the other room were two beds, an old bureau, and one chair.

"Do you go to school?" asked Nat.

"I used to go," answered Will; "but my clothes are so bad I can't go now, and mamma has no money to buy more."

Just then Mrs. Hammond came in, and after Mrs. Sprague had talked with her a few minutes she and Nat said good-by and started home.

"Why are they so poor, mamma?" asked Nat.

"Because Mr. Hammond spends his money for liquor, instead of bringing it home to buy food and clothing for them."

"Just think, mamma, Will says he can't go to

school because he has no good clothes to wear. Do you suppose that suit I outgrew last winter would fit him, and could I give it to him?"

"I think it would be about right for him, and I am glad you thought of it. You can carry it down there to-morrow. Mr. Hammond used to receive the same salary that your father has, and they had a home as pleasant as ours; but one day some one offered him a glass of wine, and he took it. He drank again and then again, until he began to love the taste of it. After that he took a glass very frequently, and soon lost his position. This is the reason their home is no longer comfortable and homelike as ours is. The only way is never to taste liquor of any kind."

That night Nat stood looking out of the window toward the village.

"I never will taste it," said Nat. "I want never to live as the Hammonds are obliged to live."

— *Child's Hour.*

LESSON XXXVIII.

ISAIAH.

" The wilderness and the solitary place shall be glad; and the desert shall rejoice, and blossom as the rose." — Isa. 35 : 1.

God's people, the children of Israel, had done wrong so many times that they were not happy. Their hearts felt sad, and they wanted some one to comfort them. When you have done wrong and feel unhappy, when your heart beats so loud you can almost hear it, when a great lump comes in your throat, how sweet it is to climb up into mother's lap and tell her all about it, while she puts her arms about you! She may chide you for having done wrong, and you feel sorry, O, so sorry! that you did the naughty thing, yet how happy you are as she whispers sweet words of forgiveness! Thus God's people wanted comfort; they wanted forgiveness; they wanted to be told again how much God loved them. Their hearts ached for this comfort and forgiveness that only God could give them, because they had sinned against him.

God knew all about his people, and he knew just how they felt. God was sorry for his chosen people; he loved them and he wished to help them. He sent one of his prophets to comfort them the best he could, and said, "Comfort ye, comfort ye my people." God taught this prophet Isaiah many things to tell the people. He wanted to help them to be better, to do no wrong, and to be happy. God told Isaiah to say, "Though your sins be as scarlet, they shall be as white as snow; though they be red like crimson, they shall be as wool." How beautiful and pure the snow is when it first comes! God said that, even though they had done so very wrong that their sins were like scarlet, yet he would make them as clean and white as the snow.

How could this be? God was going to send a little child, his own dear Son, to live upon the earth. This little child would be so good, so loving and kind, that he would help to make all those about him good and pure. The life of this little child would be so sweet that it would make all the people happy. It would comfort them; it would make their hearts so glad and happy that they would be like a wilderness where nothing had ever grown, which suddenly became full of beautiful flowers and was covered with roses. God said that the coming to the world of this beautiful little babe would bless the people so greatly that it would be like the whole country beginning to bloom and everything singing together for joy.

God told Isaiah to tell the people that the child would make weak people strong, blind people to see, deaf people to hear, and would bring comfort to all who were sad. The little babe would himself bear the sorrows and griefs of the people that they might be comforted and joyful.

I want to tell you what the good prophet said about him, "For unto us a child is born, unto us a son is given; and the government shall be upon his shoulder [that means that he should care for all the people] : and his name shall be called Wonderful, [is not that a beautiful name for him? for would it not be wonderful to have a little babe bring such joy and comfort to all the people?] Counsellor [for he should tell the people what to do], Mighty God [he was God's own Son], Everlasting Father [he would be as kind to all as any father could be], Prince of Peace [for he would bring peace and happiness upon the earth]."

Was it any wonder that the people began to look and wish for the time when the little babe should come upon the earth? How very kind of God to give them this wonderful promise to cheer them and to help them to do what was right until the child should come! The people were so sad and unhappy that they could hardly wait for the coming of the promised babe. They hardly knew what they wanted, because of the bad feelings that came from the wrong things that they had done; but they felt sure that, when God sent the promised child, all would be right.

Many years did the prophet Isaiah continue to tell the people about the wonderful child that should come, and afterward God sent other prophets with the same story. The people all believed that he would come sometime, but it seemed a very long time to wait. After a good many years some of the people almost forgot about it, but many remembered and still waited and watched and hoped and prayed for the coming of the dear little babe who would make them all happy and would help them to do right.

MEMORY GEM.

By cool Siloam's shady rill
  How fair the lily grows!
How sweet the breath, beneath the hill,
  Of Sharon's dewy rose!

Lo! such the child whose early feet
  The paths of peace have trod;
Whose secret heart, with influence sweet,
  Is upward drawn to God.
            — *Reginald Heber.*

OCCUPATION.

Have the sand-board with nothing in it but the sand. Our hearts are sometimes like the sand where nothing grows. Put into the sand beautiful sprigs of green and lovely flowers, to show how great a change God can make in the hearts through his Son.

STORY. — LITTLE JOLLIBY'S STORY.

Once upon a time there crept into fairy-land a poor little child who had never had very good times. His eyes were not very bright, because he did not have much that was bright to see, and his face was thin because he was not fed as some children are. His heart ached because no one loved him particularly well, — no one he knew of, — and he was tired because he had come a long way and it was by mistake, he thought, that he had wandered into fairy-land.

But the child was there, and was too surprised and happy to want to go away. He lay down on a bed of thick green moss, and was thinking what he would say if the fairies should see him there, and wondering if they would drive him away when all at once the fairy queen shook her wand and it was still everywhere in a minute. Then she said: "Listen to me, little spirits; there is a young stranger come to fairy-land, a young stranger with eyes and heart all full of wants. Go, little spirits, find out, if you can, what it is the little wanderer is wishing for; then come and bring me word."

Everything grew so lovely right away that the child thought it must be heaven. The gentle cup fairies carried him sweet drinks and pleasant food, and the child thought he would never be hungry again. He used to think that, if he could have all he wanted to eat, happiness would come right straight off. But now he had feasted at the fairies' table; yet he still had a great want left in his heart. So the cup fairies went and told the queen.

Then she shook her wand again, and the breath from somewhere set the silver white harps playing, and the song fairies poured out their lovely songs and the air was full of music. The child thought again it must be heaven; but after hearing the prettiest songs the little fairies could sing there was still a great want left in the little child. So they had to go and tell the queen.

She held up her wand again, and flocks of glancing midges danced on cobwebs. Splendid little birds of blue and gold twittered close by, and let the child look into their lovely eyes. They sung to the patter of the midges' feet, and everything in fairy-land did its best to please the child. But still his heart wanted more. So the midges and the birds and the fairies had to go and tell the queen.

She stood up on her pretty throne, and it was as still as still could be. "My little spirits," she said, "we can't satisfy this child that has come to fairy-land. We have fed him, danced and sung for him. But hear me; there are things that fairies cannot do until they meet the true spirits sent on the errands we all know about, and get them to help us."

It grew so still that not the tiniest thing stirred. In the air were lots of fairies that stopped flying when the queen rose on her throne, and there they stayed, their wings all spread, the little feet all quiet. The harps shone white and bright, but did not make a sound. Everything was listening. Even the midges peeping out of the flowers held their golden heads still and listened.

The queen's voice was very soft and low as she

said, "I must find a little bird of paradise and send a message to the Loveliest One." Then every fairy bent its sweet little head, and crossed its hands over its breast, and partly folded its shining wings.

What the child saw he never knew; no place was seen, no person came, but the sky was like one great rose, and it grew shiny everywhere. Then from one speck of the sky brightest of all, that seemed to open, something like a white angel flew right into the child's heart, and he felt all at once that if he spoke the white angel would answer.

"Where am I?" said the child.

"Close by the kingdom of heaven," said the angel.

"But I can't see it."

"No; not until the Loveliest One opens your eyes."

"Who is the Loveliest One?"

"The kind, sweet Spirit that watches the children and draws them until they love him best of all."

"But I can't see him."

"You do not need to, child; he is here all the same, though."

"But how does he know me? I'm little and poor and almost nobody in the great, great world."

"Hark," said the angel. "The Loveliest One is the Christmas Child — he who came to the world on Christmas morning. He came to save the children and every one, and wants everybody to love him. Everything good and sweet in the world comes from the Loveliest One. There isn't a child in all the wide, wide world so small or poor or lonesome but the Loveliest One knows all about it. He goes into all the rich folks' houses, into the homes of friendless children, and into the small, dark places where people think no one sees them or cares anything about them. He loves the children." — *Arranged from "Little Jolliby's Christmas," by Harriet A. Cheever. Congregational Publishing Society.*

ST. JOHN AND THE LAMB.
From a painting by Murillo.

LESSON XXXIX.

JOHN.

" The voice of one crying in the wilderness, Make ye ready the way of the Lord." — Luke 3 : 4.

Long after Isaiah lived there was a man named Zacharias, who was one of God's priests. As Zacharias was standing at the altar burning incense, the angel of the Lord stood before him and told him that he should have a son, and should call him John. The angel told him that this little son would be greatly blessed and that many people would be glad because of him. Zacharias was very happy, because he had always wished for a son, and he thought much about what the angel had said.

When John was old enough to understand about it, his father told him about the promise of the little babe that should come, who would be so loving that all the world would be better. The boy John lived out-of-doors a great deal. He often looked up into the beautiful blue sky and thought of the promise of one who would bless all the people. When he walked through the woods, he wondered when the little babe would come, and wished that he might see him.

Many of the people who knew about the promise thought that the little child would grow to be a man, and that then he would be their king. They thought he would be very rich and powerful, that he would make their nation the greatest nation upon the earth.

They forgot that Solomon, the wise man, had said that wisdom was better than riches or power.

John did not believe that the little babe would become a king and sit upon a throne. He knew that that would not make the people happy. He knew that the only way the children of Israel could be always glad and happy was by being good and kind. John thought that the little child who was to come would be so sweet and generous and good that it would help all those about him to be the same. John knew that he would be perfect; he would know and do only the good.

God put it into the heart of John to tell the people that the one who was to come would be perfect, that he would be holy and pure, that he would always do what was right. So John went from one place to another, telling all whom he met about the little babe who was to come, who would be so loving and sweet that it would help others to be like him. John also told them that, if they wished to become happy, they must try to do the right. They, too, must be loving and kind and unselfish. The little babe who had been promised could not make them happy if they did wrong things all the time. They must try to do right, and, if sometimes they did something wrong, he would forgive them and comfort them and they would be happy again. But they must feel sorry for what they had done, and try to do better the next time.

Many of the people believed what John told them, and were very glad. They tried to do what was right and to be kind and loving, unselfish and gentle, to those about them; and soon they were much happier than ever before. They found that it was the best thing to do to all about them just as they would like to be done by.

The people who listened to John and believed what

he said about the coming of the little babe began to watch and wait for his coming. They often prayed that he would come soon and that they might be like him. Some of the people thought that perhaps John was the one who had been promised, but John said, "No." He was sent to tell the people about one who should come afterward who would be much greater than he. John sometimes did wrong, even though he tried to do what was right; but the little child who had been promised would never do anything wrong. He should be all kindness and love.

MEMORY GEM.

Be good, sweet maid, and let who will be clever;
   Do noble things, not dream them all day long;
And so make life, death, and the vast forever
   One grand, sweet song.
— Charles Kingsley.

OCCUPATION.

Have an object, to represent John, wandering along in the wilderness. Let other men join him from the different villages and towns, which can be built or not as the teacher desires.

STORY.—THE NEW SONG.

Long, long ago, when little children first came on this earth, mothers used to sing to them. Mothers still sing to their little ones, for there is nothing a babe loves better than to hear its mother's voice singing. Sometimes a mother sings a hymn; sometimes she hums without any words; sometimes the song trills and warbles like a bird; but we love them all. How pleasant it is when we have been hurt, or are tired, or want to be comforted, to climb on mother's knee, feel her arms about us, and hear her sing some sweet little air! Children have always loved music, and we hope they always will.

Once a promise was given of a new song. The promise was made so long ago that no one remembers when it was given, but all the people believed it and began to listen for the song. It was to be so lovely that it would make every one happy who heard and understood it. It would make even those who were sad smile. It would make the children happy from morning till night. Sometimes it seemed to some mother as if her little child must have heard it as she looked into his happy eyes and saw his sweet smile.

The people often listened for it even when they were busy. The children listened, too. Sometimes they thought the birds would bring it. In the spring it seemed as if the bluebird had brought it, but still they must wait.

Many wonderful instruments were made in the hope that they would bring the song. Beautiful golden harps made sweet music, but the music did not always bring happiness. Many people made new music, and it was sweet and brought pleasure, but it was not the song that had been promised.

A new song seemed to come into the heart of some one, and he sung it over and over to himself until he became very happy, and then the song was gone and he could not remember it. He wondered whether that had been the song for which they were looking, and whether he had lost it. Even little children had this feeling at times.

Many years passed, and still the people waited and listened for the new song. At last a little child was born who was gentle and kind, so loving and unselfish that he made all about him happy. When he came into the room, people were glad just to see his happy face. When he went to his work, it was always with a song. At evening he would steal out of the house to the open fields and sing until all the people stopped to listen.

After a time others began to hum the same tune, until they had learned to sing it; and the more they sung the song the happier they grew. What had seemed hard to do before now became easy. They loved to make those about them happy. It seemed to them as if the sun shone all the time, and as if the birds sung sweeter than ever before, because they were so glad.

As the little child grew older, there came a new light in his face because of the beautiful song he sung. It made every one love him; it kept him from doing wrong. His mother thought much about it, and wondered whether it could be that her son had the new song for which people had listened so long. The more she thought about this, the more she hoped that to her child had come this wonderful gift. As she saw how it blessed him, how glad and happy it made him all the time, she thought it must be true. When she saw how others began to sing the song and to grow loving and joyous, then she knew that the song had really come which would sometime make all the world happy.

LESSON XL.

THE BABE JESUS.

"A little child shall lead them." — Isa. 11:6.

At length the little babe who had been looked for so long came. The people had waited so many years that some of them had grown tired of watching for the child, others had almost forgotten about it; but some were still praying for his coming, and still others thought that he would soon come because they had heard and talked with John about him.

You remember that the child who had been promised had many names given him. I am going to tell you two more of his names. They are the ones that the children know and love the best. One name is Jesus, and the other is the Christ-child.

Before the Christ-child was born, Mary, his mother, had to take a long journey with her husband Joseph. The only way the people could travel then was on horseback, on a camel, or upon a donkey, or to walk. Mary was very poor, and she had no horse or camel. The Bible does not tell us whether she walked or whether she had a donkey upon which to ride. It was many miles from Nazareth where Mary lived to Bethlehem where they must go, and Mary was very tired before they reached Bethlehem. They had travelled all day, and it was almost dark before they reached the town. They went to an inn, hoping that they could stay there for the night, but found it full. There was no room for them. A great many

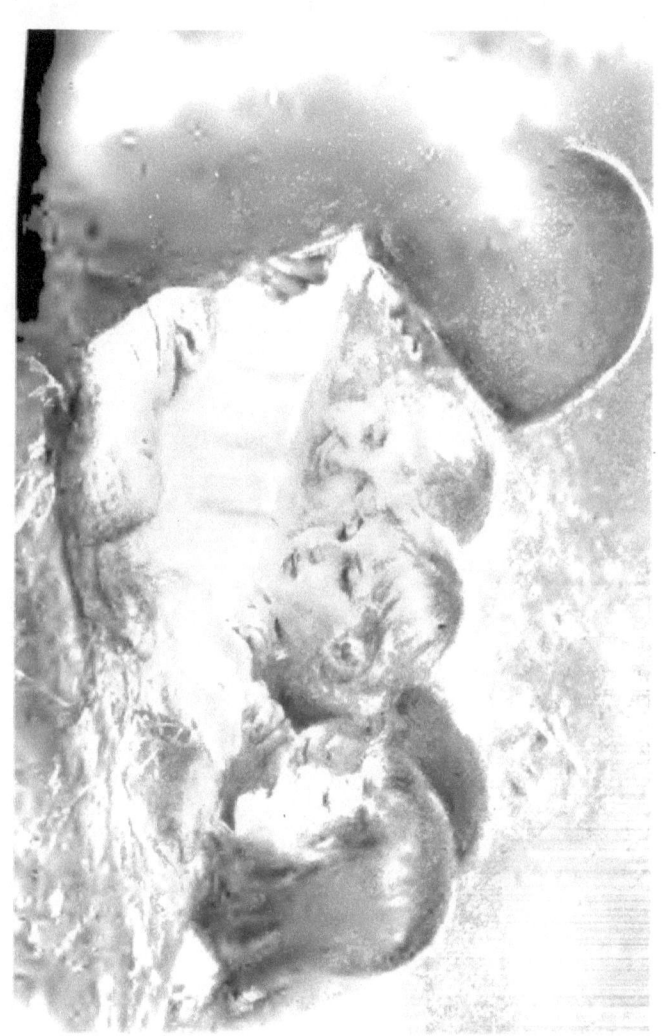

people had come to Bethlehem and wished to spend the night there. The keeper felt sorry for Joseph and Mary because she was so tired and had travelled so far. He told Joseph that back of the inn was a stable, and if they wished they could go there and lie down and rest. Joseph was very glad to find any place of rest for Mary, who was young and not very strong.

The keeper led them through the inn and up a steep hill at the back, where they found a large cave dug in the rock. There were mangers about the cave where the woolly sheep and big, brown-eyed cows were fed. Straw lay about the cave, and upon a heap Mary lay down, tired out.

And there in the cave, by and by, the wonderful baby came, the child that had been promised and whom so many were looking for.

The angels in heaven knew about the gentle child, and were glad that he had come to help the people on the earth to be good. They sung together for joy, while the stars shone brightly for they knew the Christ-child was born.

There lay the beautiful babe, with a manger for his bed, and cows and sheep about him. He looked like other babies. He was very sweet and pure, as are all little babies that have just come from heaven. His mother watched him and loved him, and by and by many people came to see him, for you know they had been waiting for him to come to the earth. The people in the inn came to see him; many people from the town came also; and even the shepherds left their sheep on the hillsides and came to the cave to see the little Jesus. When the people had seen him and loved him, they went away again, and he was left with his mother Mary, who loved him most of all.

Jesus grew to be such a sweet, wise, loving boy,

so tender and helpful, and he said and did so many good and beautiful things, that every one loved him who knew him.

He loved little children like you very much, and often took them up in his arms and talked with them. He loves you just as much now, and is just as anxious to help children to do right and to be happy as he was then. When you think of doing something wrong, and a little voice inside seems to whisper, "No, that is not right, do not do it," then you hear Jesus' voice trying to help you to be happy and good.

So the loving child was born so many, many years ago. The little babe who had so long been promised was born to make people more happy and good because he was so patient and kind, so wise and loving. The people who know him love him better and better each year. Because we are so glad that the Christ-child came on the earth, we each year remember him on his birthday. We try to make all those about us happy on that day because he has made us so happy and glad. We think his birthday the best day of all the year. It is Christmas, Christ's day, his birthday, the day when the Christ-child came to the earth. He was the best Christmas present the great world ever had.

MEMORY GEM.

Little Christ-child!
He was given on Christmas Day;
In his name let
Children give the best they may.

OCCUPATION.

Build the cave in the side-hill, and if possible make this large enough to place toy cows and sheep beside the figures to represent Joseph and Mary and the infant Jesus. Build also one or more mangers, and let the child lie in one.

STORY.—GLORY TO GOD.

One beautiful night long ago there was music everywhere. The bright stars up in the dark sky were softly singing together. The night-blooming flowers, the primrose and the honeysuckle, sung sweetly together, but so low that men never heard them. Hill whispered to hill while men and children lay asleep in their houses.

Out on the plains were the shepherds taking care of their sheep. They were used to the night world so different from what we see it in the daytime. They knew how the plants looked when asleep,—the poppy, the pink, the geranium. They often watched the night-moths circling about an open blossom and dipping down into the heart of it, sipping the honey with trembling delight. They knew the look of the dark mountains looming up against the darker sky. They watched each night over the sheep as they lay huddled together and slumbered, but they knew not of the music that floated all about them.

They heard the birds' good-night as they sleepily tucked their heads under their wings, and their glad burst of song in the morning, and even an occasional chirp in the middle of the night as one turned on his perch. Sometimes a low bleat came from a sheep or one of the lambs as it nestled closer to the mother.

The stars looked kindly down at the shepherds; the sheep lay quietly at their feet, and they talked softly together, when from the dark sky above them came wonderful, beautiful music such as had never been heard before,— "Glory to God in the highest." The shepherds started to their feet; the sheep awoke from their slumber; and the hills echoed. Where all before had seemed to the shepherds stillness and quiet, now was this glorious music, "Glory to God in the highest, and on earth peace among men in whom he is well pleased."

What did the song mean? the shepherds wondered together. The stars could have told them, or the trees or the flowers. They had been singing about it, but the shepherds had not heard them. They had been glad for joy, but the shepherds had not known. They knew that a little child, the sweetest and best in heaven, had come to this dear old earth to teach us how to be happy; they knew that God had sent his own dear Son as a baby from his heavenly home to bring us gladness.

"Glory to God in the highest," came the new song; and the angels in heaven sung also, "Glory to God in the highest;" and the stars looked down and were happy.

Ever since that time the beautiful flowers have looked up into children's faces to see whether they were trying to be like the child God had sent. When they find one unselfish and forgiving, they sing to themselves the sweet song, "Glory to God in the highest."

We cannot hear them sing, but we feel the joy in our hearts. Since the wonderful music came the stars have looked down on the earth into the children's faces as they lay asleep. Each night they have looked to see how many children have tried to be loving and gentle like Jesus, and many times have they sung, "Glory to God in the highest."

You and I, dear children, can bring a bit of the wonderful music if we try to make those about us happy. We can make music in the hearts of father, of mother, and of Jesus. When we try to do right as he did, then again the stars, the flowers, and the mountains will sing, "Glory to God in the highest."

www.ingramcontent.com/pod-product-compliance
Lightning Source LLC
Chambersburg PA
CBHW031934230426
43672CB00010B/1926